THE ELEMENTS OF SUCCESS

DAVID DELLMAN

The Elements of Success
Copyright © 2021 by David Dellman, Vintage House Publishing

For more about this author please visit https://themagicofdaviddellman.com/

All rights reserved. No part of this publication may be reproduced, distributed, or transmitted in any form or by any means, including photocopying, recording, or other electronic or mechanical methods, without the prior written permission of the publisher, except in the case of brief quotations embodied in critical reviews and certain other noncommercial uses permitted by copyright law.

For permission requests, visit: https://themagicofdaviddellman.com/

Ordering Information:
Quantity sales. Special discounts are available on quantity purchases by corporations, associations, and others. Orders by US trade bookstores and wholesalers. For details, contact the publisher at the address above.

Editing by The Pro Book Editor
Interior and Cover Design by IAPS.rocks

All Biblical quotations sourced from the King James Version.

ISBN: 978-0-578-89858-2

1. Main category—SELF-HELP/Personal Growth/Success
2. Second category—BODY, MIND & SPIRIT/Inspiration & Personal Growth
3. Third category—BUSINESS & ECONOMICS/Motivational

First Edition

OTHER BOOKS BY DAVID DELLMAN

The Christmas Garden
The Mentor's Gift

TABLE OF CONTENTS

Introduction	xi
Goals	1
Generosity	10
Gratitude	13
Service	22
Letting Go	26
My Story	29
Water	57
Fire	77
Air	87
Earth	111
Spirit	127
Conclusion	136
About the Author	139

For my mother, Nancy Dellman, who measured her success by the happiness of those she loved.

DISCLAIMER

Although the publisher and the author have made every effort to ensure the information in this book was correct at press time and while this publication is designed to provide accurate information in regard to the subject matter covered, the publisher and author assume no responsibility for errors, inaccuracies, omissions, or any other inconsistencies herein and hereby disclaim any liability to any party for any loss, damage, or disruption caused by errors or omissions, whether such errors or omissions result from negligence, accident, or any other cause.

This publication is meant as a source of valuable information for the reader, however it is not meant as a substitute for direct expert assistance. If such level of assistance is required, the services of a competent professional should be sought.

ETHER

WATER

FIRE

WIND

EARTH

INTRODUCTION

"The purpose of life is to discover your gift.
The work of life is to develop it.
The meaning of life is to give your gift away."
—David Viscott

"Hope begins when you stand in the
dark, looking out at the light."
—David Baldacci

IF YOU ARE STANDING IN the dark, I hope this book will be the light that takes you to a place of hope. If you are struggling to find your purpose or mission, this book could provide the tools you need to discover and embrace it. If you are neither standing in the dark nor wondering what your life purpose is but want to live a better, happier life, this book will give you the support you have been looking for in your quest to create it.

The lessons you are about to study are not mine. They did not originate with me. Philosophers have been discussing the meaning of the elements and their application to our lives for thousands of years. The story, however, of how those lessons impacted my experience—the story you are about to read—is unique to me. It is mine and personal.

The Elements of Success is a guidebook for living well and not only achieving what you want with your life but enjoying the journey along the way. This book is about balance. You will learn to walk between extremes in a place of harmony—harmony with yourself and harmony with outside forces that place their demands on you every day.

Some books tell us to climb every mountain and go for our dreams with reckless abandon. Others ask us to bloom where planted. There is merit in both approaches, and there is a time and place for each method. Life is sometimes about making hard choices, selecting one path and leaving another behind. Sometimes the only way to move forward is to choose, but not always. In many instances, we can have both. We can have our proverbial cake and eat it too. Having everything you dream of is often more about moderation than it is about extreme sacrifice.

Be patient and intentional about bringing balance into your life. You should climb every mountain, but you should also give all you've got to the job or career you have put your hand to do right now even if that job or career is not the one you hoped you would have.

While it may be true that we cannot chase every dream, it is also true that we can achieve far more than we may think possible. You can learn to appreciate and grow from your present circumstance. You can also change your circumstances. Knowing when to do which is one of the keys to successful living. By successful living, I mean having peace, contentment, and happiness both in the here and now and in the future. Success is not a future state; it is a present moment experience, and it can be yours when you learn to balance the elements of your life.

This book will teach you to walk in that happy place of balance and harmony that is crucial to success. We need to dream, but we also need to execute. We need to plan, but we also need to feel excited about our lives. We need balance. If you let your passion, your fire, get too far out ahead of your common sense (air), then you could end up in a dire financial state (earth), and in despair (water). I should know because I have done it not once but many times.

It is from water, our imagination and emotions, that we first encounter our dreams.

Fire inspires us to act.

Air creates the plan.

Earth gives us the grit and determination required to bring our dream into reality.

These are the elements of success, and they are a part of our mainstream culture and our heritage. When we speak of passionate people, we describe them as being "on fire." We love to say of practical people that they are "down to earth;" when we sense a trend, we say it is "in the air," and less commonly but not at all uncommon, we describe possibilities as an "ocean of dreams."

There is a fifth element, spirit, that is equally important, but in our materialist culture, it is too often ignored or marginalized. I will address the realm of spirit in the latter part of this book in a way that I hope you will find nonsectarian.

In ancient times and cultures, some personified the elements. Each element had characteristics and personality, and each was called upon at different times for different purposes. Some associated the elements with magical creatures.

The undine is a creature of the water. First named in the alchemical writings of Paracelsus, they may take many forms but are best known as mermaids. Mermaids are beautiful and artistic. They sing with an unearthly loveliness, and to a lonely sailor at sea, they can be a source of strength and comfort just as our dreams can comfort us.

Salamanders are creatures of fire. By salamander, I don't mean those cute little lizard-like creatures but a magical being. While it may have the shape of the salamander, we all know and love, the elemental salamander lives and breathes fire. They are passionate and difficult to contain.

The sylph is a being of air, a winged creature with a human shape like a fairy or angel. When they are around, they bring clarity of thought, sobriety, and decisive action. Angels are known as messengers or message carriers. So it is with the sylph.

Gnomes live in the earth. They are practical, hardworking, enterprising, and thrifty. If we are ever to make a dream come true, we need to learn the lessons of the gnomes; we need the willingness and the will to work hard.

Studying the elements and the creatures associated with each element will contribute greatly to finding the right balance in your life.

I have enjoyed three main passions in my life: writing, religion, and performing or speaking. I have known the sweet taste of success and the bitter sting of failure in all three areas. I have devoted years of effort to my dreams and often extended myself financially or otherwise in an attempt to realize a dream. While it is true that you can accomplish more when you devote your full-time energies and resources to an endeavor, the broader and less romantic question is: Is it prudent?

Is it prudent to overextend?

Is it prudent to neglect our family or our health in the pursuit of any goal?

It never ceases to amaze me how gullible I can be when I want to achieve a goal. I have told myself that I need to invest in my success by spending beyond what is reasonable. I have rationalized, telling myself that I am "investing in my future," which is not entirely untrue, but discipline needs to apply to finances as to all areas of life. When we overspend in the hope of buying a better life, we limit our ability to enjoy the life we have in the here and now.

Performance magic and my career as a speaker have been areas of vulnerability for me. I have spent thousands of dollars on props hoping the prop would make me a more attractive magician than my competition. But booking agents and meeting planners pay for a personality, not a prop. The best entertainers do not rely on a novel prop. People go to their shows or pay top dollar to book them because they like the person, not because they have the coolest prop. In the performance magic business, as in most entertainment art forms, if you can do something no one else can do or can do something better than anyone else, that distinction will get you noticed. But likability is the factor that will get you a referral or a repeat booking after your foot is in the door. You cannot buy likability. You have to earn it, and there are no short cuts.

I have made similar mistakes as a speaker, investing thousands in coaches or courses that promise a fast track to success. There is no fast track to success, and we are where we are, right here and right now, in the circumstances in which we find ourselves, because we need to be. We need to learn the life lesson of our present situation before life will give us a new circumstance. Being faithful to what you have and where you are is the best way to advance.

"Our lessons come from the journey, not the destination."
–Don Williams, Jr.

It is best to remain flexible about what we want, our goals, and our future.

Have you ever heard the saying, "Man proposes, God disposes?" It is the title of an 1864 oil-on-canvas painting by Edwin Landseer. The painting portrays an expedition gone wrong as white polar bears consume the remains of the explorers. A "grizzly" end, no pun intended, but the point is that most of us make grand plans. Those plans don't always work out the way we envisioned, and that is okay. We can learn more from our mistakes than from our successes if our attitude is right, and we can enjoy the journey along the way. Enjoying the journey is what *The Elements of Success* is all about.

I want you to be happy right now. Our culture teaches us to believe that happiness is contingent. For some, it may be contingent on going to the "right" school or marrying the "right" person or securing the "right" job, but when happiness is contingent on any outside circumstance, it is always elusive. Once we achieve what we thought would make us happy, we do not discover joy. Instead, we find ourselves looking into another horizon, another contingency, another mountain to climb to be satisfied finally.

THE ELEMENTS OF SUCCESS

Shawn Achor, author of *The Happiness Advantage: The Seven Principles of Positive Psychology That Fuel Success and Performance at Work*, said, "Happiness is the center around which success orbits." Happiness is here and now, it is not a someday when. I hope this book will give you a roadmap for living each day in a state of joy because that is what you deserve.

You have a calling, a life's work. You may already know what you want to do, have, or achieve in your lifetime. But like so many, you may have been listening to the voice of fear instead of hope. Maybe you have convinced yourself that you couldn't make a living doing whatever you long to do. Don't be afraid to fail, and don't worry about detours or course corrections. They are all part of this beautiful experience we call life.

> "Sometimes, the most scenic roads in life are
> the detours you didn't mean to take."
> – Angela N. Blount.

Enjoy the journey.

I enjoy life more when I focus on the present while keeping balanced, healthy, and realistic goals. When I dreamed of only one kind of success, when that goal was both far off and extremely difficult to achieve even under the best circumstances, my present moment was characterized by frustration and angst. I still want more from my speaking business, my performance career, and my novels and books, but I have learned to enjoy the journey, and I learned to do this by embracing the lessons the elements teach.

I consulted with a reference librarian of the Humanities

and Social Sciences Division of the Library of Congress. I needed help determining the origin of the lessons I am about to share with you. The librarian said that the "Greek philosopher, Empedocles, is thought to be the originator of the four elements teaching."

Empedocles lived from 490 – 430 BC. It may be true that a systematic teaching about the elements emerged with him, but there are references to the elements going back centuries before. Ancient astrology, which some believe originated in Egypt, associated each of the twelve signs of the zodiac with an element. I am not a historian, but I feel it necessary to show that what I have embraced as real and vital in my life didn't originate with me. People much wiser than I have been embracing what you are about to learn, and they have done it for centuries.

Listen, for example, to the words of St. Francis in his "Canticle of the Sun."

> Praised be You, my Lord, through Brother Wind,
> and through the air, cloudy and serene,
> and every kind of weather through which
> You give sustenance to Your creatures.
> Praised be You, my Lord, through Sister Water,
> which is very useful and humble and precious and chaste.
> Praised be You, my Lord, through Brother Fire,
> through whom you light the night, and he is beautiful
> and playful and robust and strong.
> Praised be You, my Lord, through Sister Mother Earth,
> who sustains us and governs us and who produces
> varied fruits with colored flowers and herbs.

Francis refers to the elements as his brothers and sisters, his family, implying that he enjoyed an intimate relationship with each. He also suggests that each element is a life-sustaining force. Francis understood the importance of the elements in his life, sustenance, and well-being, and so can you.

The periodic table lists many more than four chemical elements. As addressed in this book, the elements are not intended to be scientifically quantifiable properties but instead philosophical or spiritual principles. There is a long, even ancient, philosophic tradition of seeing our world as physical and spiritual in terms of the elements. It is this tradition that I am drawing from to form the central thesis of this book.

Throughout the ages, wise men looked to the stars for guidance. They associated the signs of the zodiac with one of the four elements, and they ascribed specific characteristics to each element. An understanding of these characteristics is an essential first step in our discussion. Still, the challenge is to move beyond the traits associated with our birth sign to cultivate those of other signs or elements in our own lives.

Too many people are fatalistic when the conversation moves to topics like astrology or destiny. We may or may not have been born with a certain predisposition, but we do have the ability to change and to cultivate those characteristics that will contribute significantly to our success or happiness.

In my case, I am a Cancer.

The sign of Cancer is associated with water. Other water signs include Scorpio and Pisces. Water people are emotionally sensitive. We are empathetic, sometimes so empathetic it hurts. If left unchecked, our sensitivity can lead to depression. Many of us are so empathetic that we may appear to be psychic. Perhaps more significantly, for our purposes in this book, water sign people are dreamers. We love to daydream and wish for a brighter future. We are most at home when dreaming. But just as "faith without works is dead" (James 2:26 KJV), dreams without hard work are dead.

I have a disposition that loves dreams but dislikes the hard work necessary to make those dreams come true. I have had to intentionally cultivate the strengths of those born under an earth sign to bring balance, success, and happiness to my life.

Life is in the doing not in the wishing.

However, as pleasurable and necessary as dreaming may be, it is incomplete and empty apart from the accomplishment of the dream. Accomplishing dreams means cultivating the characteristics of the other elements so that they are as strong and natural as dreaming.

The fire sign people, Aries, Leo, and Sagittarius, are passionate.

There is natural energy for these people that I envy. Energy is motivational. It is the fuel that gets us up from our chair and out into the world. Without energy, doing and accomplishing is incredibly challenging.

For those of us not blessed with a natural inclination toward fire, we must challenge ourselves to move, to take that first step. I have found that once I begin, energy comes, no matter how unmotivated I feel. Sometimes it requires an act of pure willpower to get beyond the comfort zone to where real change can happen. Taking action when you don't feel like it is challenging but fire people can inspire us to do just that—light a fire within and get to work. That is the single best formula for creating change in your life.

Air sign people, Gemini, Libra, Aquarius, are thinkers.

They have a natural inclination toward common sense and sound judgment. These are the intellectuals, the smart people, who see the obvious pitfalls and problems that the rest of us cannot or will not notice.

Dreaming without passion is a locomotive without fuel. It sits in the train station and never leaves. Dreaming with passion will get us moving, but without tracks to ride on, we crash and go nowhere. The air, or intellect, provides the path that will take us to our destination.

Earth sign people, Taurus, Virgo, Capricorn, are, as you might expect, "down to earth." They have the grit to keep on going when others quit. The bigger the dream, the more grit you will need if you are to see your dream manifest in the earth or the real world. Grit is what will keep your train moving until it reaches its intended destination.

If you want to be successful in the traditional sense, that is, if you are going to be an achiever, you must accomplish your goals. It is not enough to have goals or to wish or dream about what life could be like if you achieve them. To be successful, you must complete, accomplish, and win. But if you want to be happy, you must learn to be content with where you are, who you are, and what you have right now; you must learn to not only live in the moment but love the moment.

You have no other moment than right now.

Your past is past, it is gone. Your future will always be the next moment, never this one. All you have is this moment. Can you enjoy it, can you love it, and can you be grateful for it regardless of your circumstances?

Circumstances are like the carpet on the floor beneath

your feet. You were born to walk above your circumstances, not to be ruled by them. You can change your circumstances, but you can also choose your attitude right here and right now.

The natural temptation is to see the elements as steps to success. While this approach is not harmful, it is perhaps more beneficial to view the delineation between the elements as less defined. One element cannot exist in the absence of the others. One element might come to the forefront during our progression toward a goal, but that doesn't mean that the other elements are absent.

I will explore the elements in the order of water, fire, air, and earth. I will conclude with spirit. I selected this order for a reason, but at any given time, you must make an effort to incorporate each element's lessons instead of one to the exclusion of the others.

When you begin a journey, you naturally start with imagining where that journey will take you. Our imaginations are genuinely limitless. The creativity, dreams, and desires that emerge from the imagination are the domain of water. As you reflect and imagine, look for that one dream that will ignite your passion, which creates excitement and energy, inspiring you to move.

Passion, excitement, and energy are in the domain of fire. Fire is like a fuel that propels you to action. But action without a plan will frustrate and confuse. You need to make informed, intelligent decisions about where you are going and how you will get there.

Discernment and well-reasoned, informed decisions are the domain of air. Finally, without hard work, effort, and perseverance, even the best-laid plans are doomed to fail. Grit comes from the earth. The earth is dirty and hard, but if you till the soil before planting, it will yield a bountiful harvest in due season.

The elements can work together in the process of goal setting and achievement. The elements can take you from imagining to manifesting, but there is more to the elements and drawing on each to create a well-balanced life. If we only see the elements as steps to achieve our goals successfully, we miss the even more significant contribution they can make to our lives.

Interwoven through every element is spirit. What do you believe? Where are you going in an ultimate, cosmic sense? Spirit ties everything else together and gives our lives a higher purpose and meaning.

The world that we live in requires the perfect balance of the elements for survival. If water overwhelmed the earth, the population would drown. If fire consumed the air, we would suffocate, or the flames would destroy us. We need balance and harmony for optimal living conditions. In the same way, balance and harmony are also required for our success and happiness regardless of how we might individually define success and happiness.

If we have too much of one element at work in our lives to the neglect or detriment of the others, we will feel uneasy and out of balance. Likewise, if we neglect essential areas of living, even if we succeed in one or more areas, overall, we will not be content, at peace, or happy.

Before we explore the elements in more detail, there are a few foundation stones that we need to set in place so that our structure will rest on a firm foundation. At this vantage point in my life, I have the luxury of looking back on the folly of my youth and learning from it. Throughout a lifetime of struggle, I have learned to pull from and balance the forces of the elements: water, air, fire, and earth. I hope you can learn from the not so intelligent choices I have made along the way.

I don't regret a single thing that I have done; I don't regret a single choice I made with the possible exception of not telling the ones I love how much I love them while I still had them in my life. I learned from every mistake, and I have grown because of every error in judgment, but I could have benefited years ago if someone had said, "Your happiness is here and now. It is not a future state, and it doesn't depend on any circumstance. Reach out and take it."

GOALS

*"Life isn't about finding yourself. Life
is about creating yourself."*
—George Bernard Shaw

SOME PEOPLE APPEAR TO HAVE been born knowing who they are and what they want. I am not one of those people. My life has been a journey with many detours, ventures, explorations, and dreams.

What was your first and most persistent dream? What dream have you consistently returned to over the years? Why shouldn't that dream be your reality? Most of all, how hard are you willing to work for the success you want?

Perhaps you have told yourself that success in doing what you love is for other people more talented or more worthy. Talent, meaning a natural inclination or aptitude, doesn't explain success. It certainly doesn't excuse a lack of effort on the part of anyone else.

"Everyone has talent. What's rare is the courage
to follow it to the dark places where it leads."
–Erica Jong

> "Talent is cheaper than table salt. What separates the talented individual from the successful one is a lot of hard work."
> –Stephen King

> "Talent means nothing, while experience, acquired in humility and hard work, means everything."
> –Patrick Süskind

When we see a successful person and attribute his or her success to talent, it seems we disregard the hard work and effort every successful person must exert to be successful. Talent doesn't explain success. Effort does.

Some people watch an Olympic athlete and assume they had some innate gift for whatever sport they are competing in. But what we don't see is the hours, days, months, and years of persistent sacrifice and effort that led that person to the Olympic stage. We watch an actor in a great film and assume he or she was born to perform. But what we don't see is the heartbreak of rejection he or she endured to finally break through in the highly competitive field of acting. I could go on with almost any profession. The best may look otherworldly, but what they achieved was accomplished with small, incremental steps, hard work, and effort. Any dream can be yours if you are willing to roll up your sleeves and get to work.

When I was in sales, I quickly learned the value of the "numbers game." Success often comes down to the number of calls I was willing to make. I knew that I had to make X number of calls if I wanted X number of qualified leads and then had to follow up on those leads diligently if I wanted to close the deal. Selling isn't rocket science, and neither is goal setting and achievement.

The Sound of Music has always been one of my favorite musicals. I was only five when it was released, and yet I remember the day my parents went to see it as if it were yesterday. My parents rarely left me with a babysitter, but they needed a date night every now and then. So, on this particular night, a babysitter came to stay with my one-year-old brother and me while our parents enjoyed the film on the big screen as it should be seen. When my mother returned that night, she was awestruck. It was her emotional reaction to the film that made a lasting impression on me. Years later, once I too saw *The Sound of Music*, I knew why she had been so touched that night. One of my favorite scenes was when Mother Abbess, played by Mary Margaret "Peggy" Wood, sings "Climb Ev'ry Mountain" by Rodgers and Hammerstein to encourage young Maria to leave no stone unturned in the quest for her destiny. The motivational words of the song inspire the listener to pursue every avenue in the effort of bringing their dream to life.

Have you found the dream that requires all the love you can give every day of your life for as long as you live? If you haven't, don't give up. You may never know how sweet life can be until you have found your dream, purpose, and mission.

Achieving success requires effort, planning, and goal setting. In "Reflections of a Compulsive Goal-setter," Daniel Wong discusses goals, saying that a large majority of the American population—80 percent—have no goals, and only 4 percent actually have goals and look at them on a consistent basis. He goes on to state that in their lifetime, the people who set goals and continuously focus on them end up making nine times more money than those who don't.

Let's think about this. Do you want to be in the 80 percent with no goals or the top-earning and achieving 4 percent who do? If you are reading this book, I would assume you are in the 4 percent population with written goals.

Goal achievement requires time, focus, and dedication, but why should you sacrifice time with your family to achieve vocational success, or why should you sacrifice the foods you love to achieve the level of fitness you want? If you do nothing but work and sleep, your family will suffer. If you eat only ice cream, your health will suffer. But if you work hard during a reasonably long workday, then devote your undivided attention to your family when you are not at work, you may expect health and prosperity from your personal and professional life. It is not about giving up one thing entirely; it is about learning to balance multiple goals and priorities.

Goals by their very nature require discipline, and discipline doesn't always feel good, but with the proper balance, you can enjoy your life now while you strive to improve in all the areas that you believe require improvement.

One secret of success is setting clear, obtainable goals, which means small goals that add up over time. Goals are an investment not only in your future but in your present experience of satisfaction.

When you set goals, determine the incremental steps necessary to achieve those goals, then look at your schedule and resources and decide what you must do at each progressive level to ensure success. One step at a time, as you work to achieve the goal you have set, be sure to pat yourself on the back and congratulate yourself for a job well done. You are one step closer to a realized dream!

ACHIEVING THE GOALS

When working to realize your dream, you first want to establish the goals that will assist you in reaching it. Then, let's take those goals and break them down further, providing yourself with steps to take in order for you to achieve those goals.

YOUR DREAM:

GOAL 1: _____

_____

_____

Step 1: _____

_____

_____

_____

Step 2: _____

_____

_____

_____

Step 3: _____

_____

_____

_____

Step 4: _____

_____

_____

_____

GOAL 2: _____

_____

_____

Step 1: _____

_____

_____

_____

Step 2: _____

_____

_____

_____

Step 3: _____

_____

_____

_____

Step 4: _____

_____

_____

_____

GOAL 3: _____

_____

Step 1: _____

_____

_____

_____

Step 2: _____

_____

_____

_____

Step 3: _____

_____

_____

_____

Step 4: _____

_____

_____

_____

NOTES

_____

_____

_____

_____

_____

_____

_____

_____

_____

GENEROSITY

CHRISTMAS IS A FAVORITE TIME for me. One year, my mother had to be rushed to the hospital on Christmas morning. Family and friends were scheduled for dinner, but I went to the hospital to be at my mother's side so that she wouldn't be alone on Christmas Day.

I will never forget the nurse in the ICU. He had an elf costume on, and he was a "jolly old soul" even though he was working on the happiest day of the year.

As I sat next to my mother, she said, "Please don't spend your whole Christmas with me. Go out and enjoy yourself."

My mother was always more concerned about the happiness of those she loved than her comfort or her own needs. I hope some of her love rubbed off on me.

I said to her, "Mom, I'd rather spend Christmas Day in the ICU with you than spend it anywhere else without you."

The words I spoke that day proved to be so true.

She didn't live to see the next Christmas.

Later Christmas night, 2014, she asked me to get a pen and paper. When I did, she started to tell me what she wanted at her funeral. I objected. She said, "You must, Davey. I can't tell your father; he won't remember."

My dad was in the early stages of dementia at the time.

I recorded what she told me.

She passed on June 24, 2015, only days before my birthday. She always used to call me on the hour of my birth to wish me a happy birthday. The phone didn't ring that year.

I made sure that every detail she asked for on that Christmas night took place at her funeral.

My mother provided for me the most excellent example of a life lived unselfishly of any I have ever seen.

Generosity is one of many foundation stones when it comes to successful living. As a rule, the more generous a person is, the more fulfilled that person feels. If everyone looked out for number one, this world would be in a sorry state.

Be the most generous person you know, and you will also be the happiest person you know. Please resist the urge to record what people owe you or the wrongs they have dealt you. Each person is on his or her own journey. Give people the space they need to live their journey. Even better, lend a helping hand without looking for a return on your investment.

Giving to and helping others establishes trust and rapport, but "networking" shouldn't be your motive. If giving is to benefit you, you must do it without any expectation of reciprocity. The person you lend a helping hand to today may well be in the position to do the same for you tomorrow, but you shouldn't help to receive help. Instead, help someone else for the satisfaction of knowing you made another person's journey a little easier. It is a great feeling and an indispensable key to happiness.

We are here to help each other.

If you have never experienced the pure, unadulterated joy of giving, you are officially challenged to give. Consider this a call to action. Find someone who couldn't possibly pay you back and give.

Giving is personal. I cannot tell you how to do it or who to do it for, but one of my favorite joys is the annual Angel Tree. If you are not familiar with it, the Salvation Army has a program that is designed to provide children with items such as clothes and toys from birth to twelve years of age. The information about the child and their needs is listed on a paper angel and placed on a Christmas tree. From there, an individual can choose an angel and provide those items for the child. As a result, the Salvation Army has been able to help thousands of children each year during the holiday season.

While serving as a youth pastor, I delivered Angel Tree gifts and saw firsthand the impact the project has on families. I love to donate because I know it will make a child happy on Christmas morning even though I will never see that happy child.

When you give, you lift your spirit. You are happier, healthier, and more optimistic. We are hardwired to be givers. Only fear can keep us from embracing what we were all born to do: give to each other without any expectation of return. Do it today. You will be glad you did.

GRATITUDE

WHAT IF I COULD WAVE a magic wand and grant your every wish? How would having all your dreams come true make you feel? Did you know that you can choose to feel that way right now? The secret is gratitude.

When you are genuinely grateful for what you already have, you open the door to a happier life, and you lay the foundation for more. Gratitude is the fuel for success both now and in the future.

The attitude of gratitude is the most critical ingredient for personal happiness and contentment. There is no healthier attitude than gratitude. If the poorest person is grateful for what little he or she has, that person will live a contented, peaceful life. Conversely, if the wealthiest person on the planet fails to appreciate his or her wealth, feels entitled, or focuses instead on what is lacking, that person will not find happiness.

If happiness is a city on an island, gratitude is the bridge that carries us over.

You may have received terrible news. Maybe you lost a job or a gig you were sure you were going to get, maybe your pipes broke in the basement, and family heirlooms were water damaged. Perhaps you had a frightening report from your doctor. Whatever the circumstance, good or bad, you can choose to walk above it. Let your attitude be one of gratitude in sickness and in health, in wealth and in poverty.

A choice to be grateful is a choice to be happy.

When you choose to be grateful, you are choosing to enjoy the journey. Gratitude is the secret of a happy life. You will not be happy when you achieve your dream goals if you are not happy now.

Those who are grateful for what they currently have are infinitely more satisfied with their lives than those who continually yearn for more. There is nothing wrong with ambition if it doesn't rob you of joy in your present moment.

We need balance; we need the energies of all four elements, not just one, and those energies must function harmoniously. Too much water and you are a dreamer who never works, too much fire and you will soon exhaust your energy, too much air and you will be paralyzed in thought and analysis, too much earth, and you will never see the sky.

The value of gratitude cannot be overstated, and there is a direct correlation between our sense of gratitude and our happiness. We cannot be genuinely happy in the absence of gratitude, and where gratitude is present, there is happiness. So, if it is happiness you seek, meditate on what you are truly and deeply thankful for, and this elusive thing we call happiness will come to rest upon your shoulder.

You might accomplish every goal you set for yourself, but unless you are grateful for what you have, your achievements will not bring you happiness. You might earn more, you might have more, you might become more than you ever expected, but until you are grateful, happiness will be elusive.

The sincerely grateful are the happiest people on earth. Be one of those people starting right now.

Here is another call to action: Create a list of the things you appreciate and are deeply grateful for in the following provided space. After completing your list, meditate on it until you feel the joy and happiness you deserve welling up inside of you. Once you are done, please continue reading!

THINGS I APPRECIATE

___
___
___
___
___
___
___
___
___
___
___
___
___
___
___
___
___
___

WELCOME BACK.

I hope you are happier now than before you did the exercise.

Gratitude, like forgiveness, happens in motion. If we over-analyze how to achieve it, we will quickly give up, but if we simply start, our small steps will develop into a habit and the habit into a lifestyle. Start by making the decision that you will be grateful, that you will find something to be grateful for every day.

My favorite time to do this is in the morning. As I drive to the office, I pray, and as I pray, I remember the things and people I am most grateful for and appreciate. My mood changes, and I almost invariably start my day on a positive note with gratitude instead of fear in my heart.

The next section gives many different quotes about gratitude that emphasize its importance. The wisest people of every age have recognized this as the single most important attribute to your sense of happiness and success.

"Gratitude turns what we have into enough."
–Anonymous

"Gratitude is a powerful catalyst for happiness. It's the spark that lights a fire of joy in your soul."
–Amy Collette

"Gratitude makes sense of our past, brings peace for today, and creates a vision for tomorrow."
–Melody Beattie

"Thankfulness is the beginning of gratitude."
–Henri Frédéric Amiel

"Happiness cannot be traveled to, owned, earned, worn, or consumed. Happiness is the spiritual experience of living every minute with love, grace, and gratitude."
–Denis Waitley

"It is only with gratitude that life becomes rich."
–Dietrich Bonhoeffer

"Gratitude is when memory is stored in the heart and not in the mind."
–Lionel Hampton

"Gratitude is not only the greatest of virtues but the parent of all others."
—Marcus Tullius Cicero

"We often take for granted the very things that most deserve our gratitude."
—Cynthia Ozick

"Gratitude will shift you to a higher frequency, and you will attract much better things."
—Rhonda Byrne

"The root of joy is gratefulness."
—David Steindl-Rast

"Gratitude unlocks the fullness of life. It turns what we have into enough, and more. It turns denial into acceptance, chaos to order, confusion to clarity. It can turn a meal into a feast, a house into a home, a stranger into a friend."
—Melody Beattie

"Gratitude for the present moment and the fullness of life now is the true prosperity."
—Eckhart Tolle

"Gratitude is riches. Complaint is poverty."
—Doris Day

Gratitude is a habit.

We can create habits.

Developing any habit requires a dedication to regular practice. Think of what might be necessary if you wanted to learn to play an instrument with proficiency. Daily practice is required, not binge practicing, but dedication to a once or twice a day session. The same is true of gratitude. You must consciously practice it daily to become good at it.

Here are some steps you can take:

- Meditate – general meditation is good, but pause each day to reflect on what you are grateful for and find things to be grateful for, including your health, home, livelihood, and friends and family.
- A gratitude journal – write about the things you are grateful for in a dedicated journal every day. Go back and read this journal regularly.
- Keep a gratitude bank – this can be a jar or box or even a traditional piggy bank. Whenever something comes into your life that gives you joy, create a little note of gratitude for it, and drop that note in the bank. In so doing, you will be making deposits toward a happier life.
- Be a good finder – look for the good in others, be liberal and generous in your praise, and compliment others.

These are only a few of the concrete steps you could take to cultivate the attitude of gratitude in your life. Choose at least one of the above to commit to each day. You could also create your own way, but do devote yourself to the discipline and habit of gratitude. You will be glad you did.

SERVICE

*"Try not to become a man of success, but
rather try to become a man of value."*
–Albert Einstein

*"You can get everything in life you want if you will
just help enough other people get what they want."*
–Zig Ziglar

I LOVE QUOTES, AS YOU HAVE probably guessed, but the above two are in my top ten. The Albert Einstein quote is at the top of my goals sheet. I look at it every day. I first heard the Zig Ziglar quote when I was in my early twenties. I didn't understand it then, but the older I get, the wiser those words seem to me. Zig was a great one, and if you can get your hands on his recordings, please do.

Life is not about what we acquire but what we give. What we focus our attention on not only determines who we are, but it also determines our emotional state in the present moment. The attitudes expressed in the quotes above direct our attention and focus away from ourselves to others. When we focus on what we can do for others, we become happier, healthier, and paradoxically, more successful.

Life is about service.

An excellent example of how a service attitude works is in a networking situation. I attend my monthly Chamber of Commerce meetings. Most of the people there are selling something. I meet stock and insurance brokers, real estate agents, lawyers, and politicians. In that situation, it is easy to make conversation because everyone thinks of everyone else as some kind of prospect. My approach is to listen. I want to find out what I can do to help the person I am speaking with achieve their goals. Eventually, the person might take an interest in what I do, or possibly not, but either way, I seek to serve.

This service first attitude establishes a comfortable rapport and, eventually, trust. In the context of a well-established relationship in which I am known and trusted, who do you think the person will turn to when they need my service?

Our happiness will be in direct proportion to our service.

As I walk into my office every day, I say the same prayer or affirmation. I ask that I will be more sensitive to those I meet during my day. I pray that my eyes will open to their need and that I will do what I can to meet that need. As I interact with each person, I silently ask, "What is this person's need? What does this person want?" and most importantly, "How can I be of service?"

When you interact with people in your business or your private life, make it your discipline to set your agenda aside and focus instead on the people you are engaging. They want to connect with you. Every person has a story to tell. Make it your business to find out what that story is, and if you have a resource they need, offer it.

Eye contact is essential when it comes to service. Don't

let your eyes or attention wander. Look at the person who speaks to you, lean forward, and nod if you understand what he or she is telling you.

Active listening is a skill often hyped but seldom implemented. Like any skill, it might feel strained or artificial at first, but the more you practice it, the more active listening becomes your default response. I often repeat back or paraphrase what a person is telling me. When I provide this kind of communication, it helps to clarify my understanding, and it demonstrates my interest. To make sure I have heard and understood, I might say something like, "If I understand you correctly, what I hear you saying is this…" Then, I will paraphrase what they have told me. Sometimes a person will say, "Oh no, I meant this." It always helps to be sure.

Active listening also allows you to show appreciation for the contribution the other person is making. Try saying, "Thank you so much for sharing that with me." Or, "Thank you for including me in this discussion," etc. The development of active listening and good eye contact are skills that improve over time. Like any muscle, the more you exercise them, the stronger they get.

Service is what life is all about. When you find the service you were intended to offer, the doing of it will fill you with joy and deep personal satisfaction. Some people think work was the result of the fall, a consequence of sin. Not so. Work was given to Adam and Eve before the fall. Work is satisfying, or at least it can be when we find the work we were meant to do.

Ask yourself, "How can I be of value? What do I have to offer, how can I be of service?"

There is no greater joy than the joy that comes from offering a service to your fellow human being that will enrich that person's life. Service is a win/win. The one you are serving gains by receiving, and you win by giving.

Rightly understood, every job and every career is a customer service or sales career. Remember Zig Ziglar said, "You can get everything in life you want if you will just help enough other people get what they want."

If you are continually asking, "What can I do for the people around me? How can I make their lives better?" you will find the meaning you seek.

LETTING GO

"The comfort zone is where dreams go to die."
–Alexi Panos and Preston Smiles

"Life begins at the end of your comfort zone."
–Neale Donald Walsch

ONCE, WHEN I WAS EIGHT years of age, there was a single evening in which the whole family had vivid dreams. We spoke of them around the breakfast table in the morning, and we were all astonished when we heard the story of each other's dreams. I had several vivid dreams that night, and each one has had an impact on my life.

There is one that I would like to share with you.

To place the dream into its proper context, I was a pillow hugger, like the Peanuts character, Linus, who never went anywhere without his blanket. Around the house, I was rarely seen without my pillow. In my child's mind, it was important to me. It was my security, and I believe in the dream it represents whatever it is that gives us a sense of security. As an adult, it might be your investments, your real estate holdings, or your 401K; it might even be your job. We all have things that we cling to that make us feel safe and secure.

In the dream, I was falling.

I hugged my pillow tight to my chest with both arms tightly wrapped around it, but I fell into a deep, dark pit. As I plummeted down, I saw that there was, in fact, a bottom to the pit. At the bottom was a lake of fire.

I looked up, and at that moment, an angel flew into the pit after me.

I stretched out a hand to him.

He reached for me, and our hands met.

For the first time, my descent slowed.

His mighty wings were fanning warm air across my face.

"Reach for me with both hands," the angel said. "Let go of the pillow."

I could cling to my treasure or reach for the angel with both hands and survive.

In the dream, I fell. I bounced on the bed when I woke up.

But I never forgot that dream, and I often examine my motives. Am I clinging to a false sense of security because I am afraid of a challenge that my life offers me? Knowing when to cling and when to let go is one of the great challenges of life. In the words of Jessie Potter, "If you always do what you've always done, you always get what you've always gotten."

I am not going to advise you to go for your dream at all costs. I have done that, and it didn't work out well. I have spent thousands of dollars I didn't have and countless years chasing dreams. On the other hand, fear can keep you from realizing your dream, a better life, and happiness in general.

This book is about balance.

It is not prudent to make foolish decisions on the one hand, but yielding to fear is a recipe for a life of bondage on the other.

If you want to change and there is a good chance you do if you are reading this book, then maybe it is time to let go of whatever is holding you back so that you may reach for your destiny with both hands.

MY STORY

"A man who limits his interests limits his life."
–Vincent Price

I AM NOT A PERSON WHO always dreamed of just one thing.

I have always envied the people who wanted one thing when they were kids, then grew to realize that one dream. I like the idea, but I believe my life is more abundant for the diversity of interest areas and passions I have enjoyed. Whether or not I would have been more successful if I had focused on only one thing is debatable. It also depends on how you define success. For me, success is a life enriched by many passions. It helps to be financially well off, but I wouldn't trade joy for riches.

My story is more like a tree with many branches or a road with several detours and yet however lost I may sometimes feel internally or appear to others externally, I have invariably concluded that given a choice, I wouldn't have it any other way. There is nothing I would do differently.

My primary passions have been spirituality, performance magic, writing, and public speaking, not necessarily in that order. However, my curiosity in spiritual matters does take precedence over all other pursuits most of the time. These general areas of interest have consumed my attention throughout most of my life.

I might have made more money if I dedicated my life to one thing. I might have been recognized as an expert if I had only one mission, but I would have missed out on so much that has given my life purpose and meaning.

Each interest area has enriched my life. I wouldn't trade the experiences I have had while pursuing my interests for a handsome salary or a cozy pension. I am a curious person, and I love learning for learning's sake. Not everyone values the pursuit of what stimulates the curiosity over financial gain, but I have valued learning over monetary goals for most of my life.

Mainstream wisdom encourages us to define who we are rather narrowly and do so early in life. We tend to ask our children, "What do you want to be when you grow up?" There are many amazing and inspiring life stories from those who elected to excel in only one thing.

Consider Olympic athletes, sports stars, actors, and politicians. Many of those who have outstanding careers in these areas are known for little else; many, but not all. The pursuit of one thing to the neglect of all other interests is so prevalent in our culture that I often thought I should choose; in fact, I have felt pressure to choose. But succumbing to external pressure or social norms or even conventional wisdom will not always be in your best interest. You get to determine what success looks like for you. You decide, and no one else. It is your life; only you can define it.

The emphasis of this book is on balance, balancing the forces of water, fire, air, and earth, balancing your interests and passions with real-world responsibilities, and balancing your time and focus to achieve success and happiness.

I wouldn't be happy if I left behind the interests, passions, and pursuits I love, and I would be a lesser person.

"You'll be a jack of all trades, master of none," I have heard people say.

Do you remember when the term "Renaissance man" was a compliment, when a liberal arts education was encouraged because electing a major too early was considered a danger to a broad, well rounded, and healthy education?

I remember when educators encouraged a liberal arts education at the undergraduate level and more focused education in graduate school. I realize that educational costs are astronomical, disproportionately higher today than when I was working on my undergraduate and graduate degrees. However, I would still encourage young people to keep an open mind and resist the urge to settle on a major too soon. Students today, as in any period, need to give themselves time to explore, study, learn, and grow before settling on a major.

A Renaissance man or woman, by the way, is a person with many talents or areas of knowledge. At one time, a broad array of interests was championed and encouraged. I would like to see a return to the Renaissance value. I would like to see people pursue their interests instead of writing them off as a waste of time before they have adequately explored them. Of course, there will be dead ends. You may pursue something for months, even years, before losing interest altogether, but you will never forget the contributions that pursuing your passions will make to your life.

It is not all about the outcome.

Every passion doesn't have to be income-producing.

I have been interested in figure skating for decades. My interest was first sparked by the gold medal performance of Dorothy Hamill during the 1976 Olympic Games. After seeing her skate, I couldn't wait to get out on the ice. I was terrible. Over the years, I practiced, I even hired a coach, but I have never skated to the proficiency of even local competitive skaters. I will never be an Olympic skater, but I watch the skating events at the Olympics with an appreciation that can only come from being on the ice. When I am on the ice, I enjoy it, I forget about whatever it is that weighs on my mind, and I feel energized and renewed.

Archery is much the same for me.

I love shooting my bow. In competition I do okay, but I am not great. I do it because I love it and the doing of it enriches my life.

Explore your tangential interests.

Don't wait for permission, for the time to be right, or for some financial future to allow you some leisure time. Do it now, and you will be happier for it. Some of the most rewarding discoveries of my life came as I traveled the back road instead of the highway.

Diversity of thought and interest has enriched my life, and I think it will do the same for you.

Besides my primary passions, I also love motorcycles, photography, carpentry, and vintage home renovation. As a child, I often sat and watched a TV show or movie, not because I was interested in it, but because I knew someone else had invested their time and energy to create it, and I wanted to see if I could understand why. I watched some fantastic programs that children usually don't watch, I learned, and I grew.

I spent the vast majority of my elective credits as an undergraduate in the cultural anthropology department because other cultures fascinated me. I loved the feeling of mind expansion I experienced when I was finally able to look through the lens of a radically different mindset from my own.

I have had four passions, not one, for as far back as my teen years, and some go back further. Could I have accomplished more if I had selected only one as the focus of my life? Maybe, maybe not, but I certainly would have missed out on the life-giving experiences I have encountered in the pursuit of other interest areas.

I cannot argue against the effect of concentrated effort. I cannot dispute the story of someone else when they say their life was about one thing. I can say that my life has never been about one thing, and I believe I am better for it.

I have had other dreams along the way.

After the lunar landing of Apollo 11, I dreamed of becoming an astronaut. That dream remained passionate until, during my high school years, I interviewed with the Air Force ROTC. At that point, I was told that I was too short and too blind (nearsighted) to become a pilot.

I didn't have the instinct to persist in the face of naysayers when I was in high school. The ability to persist is grit. Grit is rightly associated with the element of earth because earth equates to hard work. Some seem to be born with grit, others develop it over time and sadly, some never develop it, but it is essential if any dream is going to come true.

There will always be someone or something standing in

your way. As a teenager, I respected the opinion of an Air Force officer in uniform who told me I would never be a pilot and, therefore, never an astronaut, so I let that dream go. Still, my dream to pastor, lead people spiritually, teach them in the weightier matters of life, and be there for them in the difficult moments of their lives has never faded.

My dream to write novels and books that inspire has never faded. My desire to produce wonder has never waned, and my desire to inspire through public speaking has never faded. These are my dreams, and I have tasted varying degrees of success and failure in each area of interest and passion.

In these four key areas, I have persisted not so much because I am determined but because I love speaking, performing, and writing so much that someone else's definition of success or failure simply doesn't matter. It is easy to persist when you love what you are doing. One of the critical ingredients of a life of happiness is spending time with the people you love and spending time with the interests and passions that you love.

I am a pastor by nature, and I always will be regardless of my current vocation.

I write because I love the process of putting my thoughts down on paper. It often seems that someone else is writing through me, and I am merely a spectator or observer. If you have as much fun reading my material as I have writing it, you will love my work.

Speaking feels much the same as writing to me. At times it is as if I am seated in the front row watching as someone else speaks through me.

Performance magic is a little different. I enjoy the

study and preparation more than the performance, which, I believe, is a primary reason why performance magic has never produced the income for me that I know it is capable of producing.

One lesson of this book is to concentrate on developing the characteristics of the elements in which you are weakest. Study and prep time is closely allied to dreaming, my strong suit, whereas performing is closer allied to earth, my weakest element. No one ever excelled in magic who didn't perform regularly. No great speakers ever became great by speaking only occasionally. Without doing, dreaming is pointless. It might have entertainment value, but until you do, until you accomplish your dream, you will never really know how that dream tastes or feels.

Dreaming without doing is like water without a glass; it makes a mess.

Do you remember the dream I had about falling into a pit?

We have all had those dreams. We have all dreamt about falling, but I plummeted toward a lake of fire in this dream. I was free-falling down a dark hole, rounded stone walls speeding past. There was nothing to grab onto, nothing to break my fall and save me from the fire below.

For me, that dream was a life warning, and it can be for you too.

Am I clinging to the things that give me a sense of security to the detriment of my wellbeing? Should I let go of my security blankets, whatever they may be, and cling with all I have to The Dream? Do I want to hold onto what makes me feel safe even if it leaves me less safe and less secure than reaching for that which can benefit me? Am I not fully committed to my spiritual journey? This dream has meant different things to me at different points in my life.

To this day, I wonder about that dream, and it remains as fresh in my mind as it did those many decades ago when I first experienced it. In this book's context, I do believe it relates to fear as opposed to faith, inaction as opposed to action.

As you pursue your ideal life, you will have to make a choice, take a risk.

Will you take the chance, or will you play it safe?

I am not going to tell you which to choose. I don't think anyone can. There will be times when it will be prudent to play it safe and other times when playing it safe will mean missing out on an opportunity that may never come again. Only you can discern one from the other for your life.

WRITING

WHEN I WAS EIGHT YEARS old, I watched *The Mysterious Island* (1961). As the credits scrolled by at the end of the film, I saw "Jules Verne's *Mysterious Island*" in the credits. I asked my mother what that meant, and she explained that Jules Verne had created the story.

She was the first person to explain what it meant to be a novelist, a storyteller. From that moment, I wanted to write stories; I wanted to capture the imagination the way Jules Verne had captured mine.

I composed my first short stories when I was eight years old. By the time I was eleven, I had written my first novel.

I remember drafting a handwritten cover letter to Bantam Books. I sent it off with some also handwritten sample chapters. Within a couple of weeks, I received my first rejection notice. They told me that they didn't accept unsolicited manuscripts. I have collected many rejections letters since that first one.

I still write, and as long as I am able, I will continue to do so. It doesn't matter how many rejection notices I collect.

Rejection never extinguishes my fire, my passion for writing. I write because writing is as natural to me as breathing.

I want to be read. All writers want to be read. In that sense, I write for others, I write as a service to my world, but it doesn't take grit for me to write. For me, writing is natural and sustaining.

I finally published a novel, *The Mentor's Gift*, in 2006. It took me three years to write that book. I worked on it after I came home from work every night.

The characters in the book became my constant companions. I loved the process. I would sit down at my computer after dinner in the quiet of my study. I would start with a page or two that I had written the day before. I would do a little rewriting, but once the characters and scene came alive to me, I would keep going until I was exhausted, which was typically about three hours. Throughout the night and the next day, the characters would continue to speak to me, and I would take notes for my next writing session. This process continued every day for three years.

Once the book was ready, I submitted it to over 50 publishers. Some were interested, but they wanted changes that I didn't want to make. I felt the changes they asked for impacted too severely the story I wanted to tell. Almost every one of the 50 publishers I solicited responded, many with detailed notes of their thoughts, comments, or suggestions. I also sent the manuscript to agents. Not a single agent responded to me even with a rejection notice.

Self-publishing was in its infancy at the time. The more comments I read from publishers, the more I realized that my novel had a unique and very narrow niche. I was going to lose that niche for a mainstream publisher, or I was going to publish it myself.

A good reason to self-publish is that you are writing for a niche that a mainstream publisher doesn't want to risk. I opted to publish it myself, and I have absolutely no regrets. I would have regretted losing my niche. I clearly could have sold more copies if I had made the changes several publishers were asking me to make, but I had a specific audience in mind, and when I finally did publish the book, that audience received it with open arms.

To this day, one of the happiest moments of my life was when I saw the cover for the first time. That was happiness like I had never known before. I had wanted to be a writer since I was eight years old. I finally held in my hands the tangible evidence that my dream had come true.

There is no feeling like the one that comes from seeing years of hard work and effort finally realized, finally real. Dreaming, the domain of water, is fun, but seeing a dream born in reality is breathtaking. You will never forget those moments. There is no joy greater than when, after all your hard work, effort, and perseverance, a dream (water) finally takes shape in the real world (earth).

Carrying a dream from its birth in water to its manifestation on the earth is the task of fire (passion) and air (intellect). You first see the dream in water; then you get excited about it, and that excitement, that fire, fuels effort.

The first effort you make is a good plan, the domain of air. Executing the plan and then finally seeing that plan achieved, this is what earth, grit, is all about.

PERFORMANCE MAGIC

MY FATHER'S FATHER WAS A lover of magic.

He instilled that love in my father, who, in turn, instilled it in me.

My grandfather, Raymond, was a traveling salesman. He sold Willcox and Gibbs sewing machines, mostly to commercial shops. Granddad spent most of his week on the road and away from his family. He wanted to make the most of the precious time he had with his family so when Grandfather finally did come home, he brought tricks with him to entertain his two children, or he would take them to a show or on a trip to the shore or Bonnie Blink, a local Masonic garden spot.

My grandad passed from this world when I was still an infant, but my father raised me on stories of the wonders my grandad used to perform.

"He came home from a long trip one year," my dad told me. "My sister and I rushed to greet him in the foyer. After a hug, he asked us to stand back, then he held his coat down so that it covered his legs and feet. He lifted the coat, and one leg was gone, then he lowered it, and when he lifted it again, the vanished leg had returned, but now the other leg was gone. Then he lowered his coat, and when he lifted it a third time, both legs were gone. The coat kept rising, and he floated almost to the ceiling."

I grew up on stories like that, stories my dad would tell me about his dad.

Then there were the shows that my grandfather would take his kids to see. The one I heard about more than any other was the Blackstone show at the Hippodrome. The orchestra would come up out of the floor, then recede. That impressed my father, but the two Blackstone effects he was most impressed with were the buzz saw illusion and the floating lightbulb.

"A huge buzz saw would come down through the woman," Dad would tell me. "She would scream and pass out as it sliced through her, sending sawdust all over the stage."

The images that story conjured in my young mind filled me with wonder, awe, and maybe a bit of terror.

Years later, I would see this particular illusion performed. You will not see it often because the apparatus is quite large, and most modern performers find it impractical, opting instead for the much more versatile Zig Zag illusion. But it is a thrill to see. There is no cover for the person being sawn asunder. The over-sized round blade does indeed appear to pass right through her.

As exciting as that story was, my favorite was the floating light bulb. Once again, my dad relayed to me what he witnessed in his childhood.

At one point during the show, a lamp would be brought center stage to Blackstone. The great magician would switch it on and off a few times before removing the lampshade. As the bare bulb stood glowing in the lamp, Blackstone would remove it still lit from the socket. Then, as my dad told me in his excited voice still filled with wonder years after the event, "It floated out over my head!"

"Was it still lit, Dad?"

"Yes! The house lights were dim. Most of the light in the theater came from that one bulb as it slowly floated out only a few feet above our heads."

I had never seen a live magic show when my dad told me those stories, and yet I knew I wanted, even needed, to do that, to create wonder the way Blackstone did, the way my grandfather did. Magic was my calling—okay, one of my callings.

On Christmas morning 1968, I awoke to find a magic kit under the tree. The gift to exceed all others in that wonder year, I now had all I needed to be the next Blackstone. I studied, I practiced, I learned every trick in the proverbial and literal book. I was ready.

On a cold but clear day in January, I prepared to perform my first show. You probably already guessed the venue: the dreaded third-grade show and tell.

I had dozens of tricks to perform, and as I presented each one, a kid in the front row called out the secret. The first time it happened I was annoyed, the second time I was frustrated, but by the third or fourth time I finally figured out what the class most likely already knew: this heckler got the same set for Christmas.

You might think a first-time performance experience like that might discourage me. It didn't. Instead, it only deepened my resolve to find material that didn't come from a department store magic kit. The next time I performed for my third-grade class, the heckler's mouth hung open, and his eyes were wide with wonder. When you can create that feeling for an audience, magic becomes addicting. Magic has been a lifelong passion for me.

When I was ten, my dad was the pack master for my Cub Scout troop. He hired local magician George Goebel, not to be confused with George Gobel, the actor/comedian, to entertain. George did his "Blue and Gold Show," a good show for a Cub Scout troop but not his most exceptional show. A year later, Dad took the whole family to see George's full evening illusion show, his most elegant show, and one of the last grand classic, full stage illusion shows ever produced.

At the end of the show, a lovely lady in a soft white gown walked gracefully to center stage. George was in a tuxedo with tails. He had salt and pepper hair and the traditional magician's goatee. He guided the young woman by the hand to a sofa and directed her to lie down. After a few passes of his hand, she seemed to fall asleep. Another man approached, and together with George, he covered the sleeping beauty with a white sheet.

George spread his arms over the resting covered body, and it began to rise. Two men came out to remove the sofa. The woman's body continued to rise until it floated well over George's head. He reached up, took hold of the sheet, and pulled it away. To my eyes, the woman seemed to vanish in slow motion. I saw her melt away like a warm breath on a cold day.

George pointed to the back of the theater, and the woman came running down the center aisle to the stage. That was magic, and I was forever hooked.

I came home from the show with a pamphlet explaining how to do some basic tricks. I studied that pamphlet for hours, even days, without sleeping. It contained some excellent tricks, but it didn't tell me how to levitate a human being, make her vanish while floating on air, or make her rematerialize yards from where she had vanished.

Many years later, I became friends with George Goebel. I spent hours at his home talking magic and admiring his extensive historical collection of magic's most significant artifacts.

George and I shared a love for magic's history.

He showed me pieces that belonged to Harry Houdini. Imagine touching a prop that Houdini used. But the most exciting piece for me was Thurston's cards. Howard Thurston was famous for his rising card routine. He was famous for many other effects as well, but his rising cards was a signature piece. George laid a deck of cards on the table in front of me, but he didn't tell me the significance of the cards. I could see that they were worn and old. When I picked them up, I knew immediately; I was holding Thurston's cards. It is a thrill that excites me to this day, and I am sure it always will.

If you don't love magic, Thurston's cards will not mean a thing to you. If you love magic, but you don't know the history of your art, Thurston's cards will not mean a thing to you, but if you are fully invested as I am, you will realize that I held in my hands an essential piece of magic history.

Whatever your passion, the history of your chosen field is vital. You must know where you came from to know where you are going.

What lights you up like Thurston's cards? What is or could be your Thurston's cards experience? It is fire that you are looking for, fire is energy and fuel. When you are excited, you are energized to act, and when you act, you accomplish.

THE ELEMENTS OF SUCCESS

To this day, I can sit up all night talking with close friends about magic or working alone on a show or routine and yet feel more energized in the morning than I felt the night before. When you find something that gives you life, that puts energy in as you do it instead of draining the energy out, hang onto it, pursue it.

PASTORAL MINISTRY

WHEN I WAS 14, I had a religious experience. Those in the evangelical community would call it being born again.

I have always liked the term "born again." When you are born, everything is new, old things have passed away or receded from memory, and the road ahead is fresh and inviting. So it was when I was fourteen.

I was raised in Christianity, but being raised in a religion and intuitively grasping the spiritual significance of a religion are two different things. You can have an intellectual understanding (air) without depth (water); you can have form without substance.

My early experience with Christianity was mostly form with no substance. I did have moments of epiphany when I intuitively understood what is beyond comprehension when all is right, and I am part of it all and yet separate. But before that beautiful moment in my fourteenth year, I didn't "get it."

I attended a private Lutheran elementary school where I attended chapel and had religious studies every day. I was a confirmed Lutheran, and yet I would argue that I knew nothing of Christianity until I had that experience at the age of 14.

My teenage experience was certainly an epiphany, a life-changing event, a breakthrough of intuitive rather than intellectual understanding. I felt alive. I felt joyful. I was in love with life and everyone around me. It happened in a small, country church at the edge of my town. It was a Baptist church, and that little church was pastored by a man who very rapidly became my hero and role model.

I sat in church week after week, year after year, dreaming that I could be like John, the pastor of that little church. I dreamed of preaching on Sunday, visiting the sick, baptizing children and adults, teaching Sunday classes, conducting weddings, and funerals. In short, I dreamed of being a pastor.

That pastoral dream dominated my life from the age of fourteen until I started my career as a human resource professional in 1994. I studied psychology as an undergraduate because I wanted to understand the human mind in preparation for serving as a local parish pastor.

I met my wife while an undergraduate. She was also a psychology major, and she has since distinguished herself as a fantastic social worker, primarily serving our nation's veterans.

While other people were majoring in hot market fields with promising salaries upon graduation, I thought only of ministry.

I married Janis a few weeks after graduating from undergraduate school and only a few days before we were due in Missouri to start seminary. We drove out from Baltimore to Springfield with all our possessions in my father's big, blue Oldsmobile. We had only $2,000 to our name. I didn't know how we would pay for tuition, let alone living expenses; it didn't matter; I believed that God would provide.

Once we settled into our roach-infested efficiency apartment, Janis started looking for work while I focused on my studies.

I was in graduate school but taking fifteen credits a semester because Janis wanted to graduate and get home as quickly as possible. A full time and challenging graduate workload is twelve credits. Graduate students spend many hours working outside of the classroom, but I was grateful for Jan's support, and I knew she wasn't happy in Springfield, so I was willing to work all the harder to get her home in a reasonable time.

Small town mid-western life was not her first choice.

She loved the busy city.

I loved the low cost of living and the slow pace of a small town.

Jan's parents didn't share her enthusiasm for a life of faith, as if security is ever really possible.

At one point early in our seminary experience, Jan was out of work, and we were rapidly running out of money. One Sunday, Jan's mother called with a bit of an "I told you so" lecture. Her mother told her, "Jobs don't come knocking on your door."

Only a moment later, there was a knock on our second-floor apartment door. When I opened the door, a stout, older gentleman in a cowboy hat said, "Hi, I hear your wife needs a job."

He gave my wife work, he bailed us out of a financial crisis only days before we would have run out of money, and he proved that opportunity does come knocking on your door if your heart is in the right place.

Follow your dreams.

The world makes room for those with the courage to chase their dreams, and it often seems to conspire to work things out, sometimes at the last possible moment, but always in time.

We spent almost four incredibly happy years in Springfield, Missouri, as I worked on my Master of Divinity. After graduating, I enjoyed two youth ministries, and then I became a Christian educator teaching the same class of older adults for over ten years.

At a time in my life when I had grown tired and discouraged, Janis and I were having dinner at a favorite restaurant. She looked up at me and said, "I miss it."

I said, "Miss what?"

She said, "You, when you had faith and hope."

We lose our way sometimes, even with the best dreams (water), the best-laid plans (air), and the fiercest determination (earth).

It is easy to get lost in the maze of life, to question who we are and what we believe. During those times, I find it helps to go back to the water, both figuratively and literally. Water helps me meditate, rest, relax, and dream. Once I start dreaming, eventually, one dream will find its way to the top; one dream will inspire me, light my "fire," and once that happens, my life has meaning and purpose again.

Your life will have meaning and purpose, too, once you embrace the dream that lights your fire.

PUBLIC SPEAKING

SOME PEOPLE CAN INSPIRE, MOTIVATE, and transform others using only the spoken word. Zig Ziglar was one such person. Zig was my hero and role model, and he continues to be even though he crossed over in 2012.

A few short years after my wife and I returned home from seminary, I found myself at a breaking point. I had consistently tried to land a full-time position in ministry, but I was not successful. I found an opportunity here or there, but nothing that worked.

I remember one offer in particular. The church was in the Louisiana bayou. I asked what happened to their previous pastor, and I was told, "A gator made off with their kid."

"Not to worry," I said. "I don't have kids."

Well, Janis wasn't too keen on it.

On another occasion, I made it to an interview with the board. Janis and I arrived on a Sunday to meet with them. It was far from home, so up until the interview, we hadn't met in person.

I could tell something was wrong. Everyone seemed a bit uncomfortable.

Finally, one person spoke up and said, "Based on your resume, we thought you'd be taller. We need a tall pastor here."

That comment didn't strike my wife or me as funny at the time, but it is amusing looking back on it.

After constant and continual effort to land a position in ministry, I was down and discouraged. I needed something to lift me once again. That something turned out to be Zig's book, *See You at the Top*, the first "motivational" book I ever read. I had read many books written by religious speakers, and many of them were terrific, but until that moment, I had never been exposed to the nonsectarian world of motivational speaking.

As a new fan of Zig, I decided I wanted to hear him speak live. By this time, I had been listening to tapes. In those days, we listened to cassette tapes, but I had never attended a motivational conference. It wasn't long before the opportunity presented itself. It never ceases to amaze me the number of opportunities that come my way once I set my mind to look for them.

Seeing Zig live was everything I hoped it would be.

Zig was engaging, he was funny, and he was motivational. I sat not far from the stage in a venue just a little smaller than a stadium. I am glad I saw him, not only that one time but many times. He is no longer with us, but I will carry those memories forever.

If you want to do something, see someone, or meet someone, don't wait. Seize the day, as the saying goes. We hold today in the palm of our hands. We are not promised tomorrow.

One way to create fire for your dream is to expose yourself to the very best in your chosen field. They will make the pinnacle of success look easy and effortless. Watching them will inspire you. I have found this to be true of pulpit ministry, public speaking, and magic. Beyond the performance arts, great carpenters can inspire you to be better, great business people or entrepreneurs can inspire you.

Whatever your passion, find someone whom you can look up to and admire and simply watch that person as much as possible. This is what I did with Zig. I didn't become a Zig groupie, but I did see him speak live many times. He gave me a standard toward which I could aspire.

Reading biographies of those you admire is another excellent way to set your flame burning. You need the water to give birth to your dream, but you need the energy of passion for fueling the effort required to create a plan (air) and execute the plan (earth).

Don't neglect to expose yourself to that which inspires you. Zig used to say, "People often say that motivation doesn't last. Well, neither does bathing—that's why we recommend it daily."

Your fire needs kindling. Without kindling, it will soon go out, and without fire, your dream will wither like a neglected fruit on a dying vine.

Professional speaking became a significant life aspiration for me. To that end, I went back to school, majoring in an education-related master's program. My objective was to land a job in corporate training, build a repertoire and a reputation in the corporate environment, then parlay that success into an independent speaking/consulting career.

I enrolled in a master's program in the early spring of 1994. By late spring, I had landed the job I was seeking. At the time, it was a small non-profit. The company was looking for someone who could create and deliver training, but they also needed the same person to run their human resources department.

In small companies, employees have to wear a lot of hats and be prepared to do "other duties as assigned." I was thrilled to have the opportunity. While I loved working for that company, in those early days, I didn't lose sight of my original objective.

Once I settled into a training routine, I recorded a few of my sessions and created promotional materials based on those recordings. I eagerly sent those videos out but was told time and time again by booking agents that they only wanted to work with full-time consultants. If I were serious about launching my own business, I would have to do just that. Agents didn't want to hire me, knowing I had a full-time commitment elsewhere.

In 1997 I earned that second master's degree that I had started in 1994, but I didn't leave the company. I grew fond of those I was working for and with. I became both proficient and comfortable in my job duties, and my salary increased as the company grew.

I resigned from that comfortable job in June of 2020 after 26 years of service. I left to devote myself full time to the pursuit of my dreams. I was making an excellent salary. I had a company-sponsored 401K and healthcare benefits, but I wasn't living the life I was destined to live.

Now I am living that life.

Writing the book you are reading is a part of that dream.

HAPPINESS

MIKE ROWE IS A HERO to me. I remember when he did a show for my hometown of Baltimore about local real estate offerings. That was in the 1980s, and the show was called *Your New Home*. It was a weekly on WJZ-TV, and I believe it ran for roughly 15 years. I watched it every chance I had because I love local real estate, but mostly, I enjoyed Mike's personality. Mike went on to carve out a unique "working person" brand with shows like *Dirty Jobs*.

In an interview, Mike said, "Find what pays the bills and then figure out a way to be happy doing it...The people on *Dirty Jobs* didn't follow their passion, but they were passionate about what they did." And that is a crucial ingredient to both success and happiness.

Most self-help books offer only one path to happiness and that one path is dream achievement, but not everyone wins an Oscar, brings home the Vince Lombardi Trophy, or writes a best seller.

If the only path to happiness is to achieve all our dreams, it is no wonder millions of people in America suffer from depression. We all work. Most of us need to work to pay our bills and put food on our table. Work is good, and work is sacred. Every honest job is a good job, and every worker is worthy of respect. We were born to work; we were divinely engineered for work.

Some people want to hear that we can have everything we want if we will only follow this or that simple program. Some of us will live that kind of life while others, despite following the same system diligently, will not. Your happiness doesn't depend on what you get or what you achieve unless you have chosen to make it so.

The saddest element, in my opinion, of placing too much importance in goals we have not achieved is that this can rob us of the joy of living in the present moment. Please don't be the person waiting for your life to start, waiting for Mr. or Ms. Right, waiting for that perfect job, waiting for that perfect house.

Tomorrow never comes, and when you finally achieve your dreams, they may not bring you what you hoped they would.

You hold only today in your hands. This moment is the only moment you are promised. Your life has already begun. Don't you want it to be the best it can be, not tomorrow, but right now?

There are two paths to success, and they are not mutually exclusive. One is to achieve your dream; the other is to learn to love what you already have. You can enjoy one level of success right now. The other is long term.

We can do what we love, learn to love what we do, or combine the two in a balanced and healthy way—this is what I am advocating. Learn to enjoy whatever it is that you are doing right now, but never give up on your dream.

To keep your dream alive while you devote yourself entirely to what you are doing now, you must be careful about your comfort zone.

Michelle Poler said, "The opposite of success isn't failure; it is comfort."

When asked about the secret to his success, Arnold Schwarzenegger said, "For me, life is continuously being hungry. The meaning of life is not simply to exist, to survive, but to move ahead, to go up, to achieve, to conquer."

Stay hungry, keep wanting, keep desiring; this is the realm of fire. Water inspires us with visions; air teaches us to plan, but fire fuels action. Whatever it is we want, we have to want it bad enough to pay the price necessary to achieve it.

> "If you don't get what you want, it's a sign
> either that you did not seriously want it or that
> you tried to bargain over the price."
> –Rudyard Kipling.

I hope my story has given you a few things to consider as we move on to discuss the elements.

Are you happy where you are, or are you hungry enough to want to create change? If you want change, what does that mean? Does it mean you quit your day job, or does it mean you work hard in your off hours to create the platform you need to launch the change you want?

There is no right answer, there is only your answer.

WATER

THE FIRST TIME I REALIZED the role of the elements in my life, I was sitting by a small lake in Tyrone, Pennsylvania. I was there for a family reunion which was held in a beautiful park. As I often do, I slipped away from the crowd for a little quiet time. Introverts like me tend to do that because we draw energy from solitude.

I sat on the grassy ground only a few feet from a lake. The water was so still I could see the sky above and the trees reflected in it. The sun was warm on my face, and the air was crisp, refreshing, and clean.

I had been studying the elements, so my reflections that day may not have been spontaneous. But as with so many things, there is a gulf between studying and experiencing, between comprehending and knowing. Sitting there by the water on that warm August day, I had what some call an "Ah-ha," moment. I prefer the term "epiphany."

As I sat there thinking about the elements, I suddenly felt connected to everything around me. There was no distinction between me and the tree I leaned against or the ground I sat on or the water. We were all one living thing. We needed each other. Together we were what we should be, but apart we couldn't survive.

I had the experience of deep understanding, a sense of knowing but without words. It was a euphoric experience, but in that experience, I suddenly saw in the stillness of the water before me the connection or intersection of the elements. I saw where the water met the air and the earth, and warming them all to the perfect temperature was the warm sun above. I saw how dependent the elements are on each other and how conditional my existence was on them. Without any one element, I couldn't survive, and neither could they, but if I understood the connection and built upon it, not only would I survive, I would thrive.

The elements are more than life-sustaining; they are life-enhancing.

It is so easy when you look at a scene like that, a lakeside view, to assume that the elements are distinct. You see the lake. It is not the air, and it is not the earth, so it is natural to think they are separate and yet one couldn't exist apart from the other, and we couldn't exist apart from them. When you experience this interdependence, this unity of all there is, you are on the right path to fully integrate the wisdom of the elements in your life. You cannot get there if you don't physically interact with them. It is easy to do. They are all around you every moment of every day.

The best way to become aquatinted with the characteristics of an element is to spend time with it. Go to a body of water. If you don't have access to a body of water, fill a glass or bucket with water. You need to interact with the elements to draw their wisdom into your life if you are to benefit fully from this study, so please don't let this be an imaginative exercise or one you gloss over on your way to the "good stuff." This is the good stuff.

So, go out and find a body of water. It could be a small lake or an ocean. Whichever you choose, sit by it, preferably in a meditative state of mind, and ask the water to speak to you. If that sounds too mystical or impractical, simply reflect on the qualities of water and how you might integrate them into your life.

Imagination is to water what hard work and effort are to the earth. Imagining is the fun part, but imagining without ever seeing what we imagine come to pass is a promise unfulfilled. We tend to live in a perpetual state of frustration if all we ever do is imagine.

> "Imagination is the beginning of creation. You imagine what you desire, you will what you imagine, and at last, you create what you will."
> –George Bernard Shaw

> "Where there is no vision, the people perish."
> –Proverbs 29:18

Vision can keep us alive amid the most devastating circumstances. Vision and hope are much the same. If you are one of the few people who has never read Viktor Frankl's *Man's Search for Meaning*, then by all means, please get your hands on it and read it. I read it as an undergraduate psychology student, and it changed my life. It was then and continues to be one of the most important books I have ever read.

Viktor Frankl was a man who had everything then lost

everything, but in that state of utter despair, instead of giving in to hopelessness, he reached for something greater, for meaning even amid the chaos, and he found it. He is the father of logotherapy, meaning, and the significance of meaning to the human soul.

Imprisoned at Auschwitz and other concentration camps for three years during the Second World War, Viktor Frankl began to wonder why some around him survived while others perished or gave up. He found that, "Where there is no vision, the people perish." Where the people he was surrounded by at Auschwitz had hope, they tended to survive, whereas those who gave up hoping tended to perish. There was no difference in the circumstances of those who had hope and those who did not. They were both in arguably the worse possible living conditions, and yet some persevered while others gave in.

It was their dream that gave meaning to their lives.

It was their dream that gave them hope.

Have you ever been told to stop dreaming and get to work? There is undoubtedly a time to do just that, but there is also a time to dream, and dreaming should never be undervalued, for it is the lifeblood of all achievement, of existence itself.

Never underestimate the power of your dreams.

Some believe that all life emerged from the sea, and water is known as the realm of dreams and desires. It inspires us to imagine in vivid detail a positive future state.

Everything in your life—your vocation, a relationship, a belief system, or a possession—began with a thought, an idea, a dream. And dreams originate in water, in your imagination. You must see it before you can achieve it. The more clearly you see it, the more tenaciously you cling to your vision, the more likely you will achieve it.

One of my favorite films is *Flashdance*. I have a great many favorite films, and I realize that *Flashdance* is hardly the pinnacle of artistic achievement in the motion picture industry, but the film had a simple yet profound message: "When you give up your dream, you die." In other words, without a vision, we will perish. We may not physically die, but on some level, we stop living when we give up on our dreams. Our zest for life is gone. It is hard to keep a fire burning without wood to fuel it, and it is hard to be excited about living without dreams.

One day, my wife and I were having dinner at a favorite restaurant. Suddenly, she looked up and said, "You know, I enjoyed life more when we had dreams and hope." We laughed at the moment, but what she said was sobering. She had gone through four years of seminary at my side to graduate with no prospects. After years of trying, I gave up, I failed. Then I became consumed with a vision to be a performer, a magician. I worked at that dream for 15 years but never saw the success I was hoping to achieve. In the context of these two apparent failures, we sat at that table where she made that comment.

How important is a dream? How important is it to wish to be, do, or have more, to achieve more? It is much like a plant that never grows or a sun that never shines.

Have you ever gone fishing? Have you ever watched the thin line of your reel reach down into the murky water? I remember sitting for hours on warm summer days. I didn't care if I caught anything. I simply enjoyed being by the water. But then I would invariably feel a tug, and suddenly a lazy, restful summer day turned into a nail-biting battle. I would give the line a good stiff yank to sink my hook into the fish; I would pull, then let out, then pull again and begin to wind. I couldn't see the fish, but I could feel the resistance and movement on the other end of the line. Finally, when I reeled that fish up into the air, I could see what I had caught.

The water held the fish, the sun kept me warm and comfortable, and the earth gave me a solid footing. The air let me see what I had caught, but no one fishes in the air. Fish live in the water, and so do your dreams.

There are few places I love more than Ocean City, Maryland. I take a trip to the beach at least three times each year. I love to stand near the ocean and look out over the apparent limitless sea.

People talk about the "ocean of dreams" or the "sea of emotion." Water speaks to us of emotion but also of potential. Life does indeed emerge from the sea. Your life will begin with your imagination. What do you imagine for yourself? What do you dream of being or doing? How do you feel when you hold those dreams in your mind? This is the element or the domain of water.

We each have an element in which we feel the most comfortable. Water is my element. I could spend my life dreaming, and without intentionally cultivating the characteristics of the other elements in my life, that is precisely what I would do.

Earth people often resist dreaming. They are too "down to earth" to spend time in such a frivolous activity as dreaming. "Why waste time dreaming when there is work to be done?" you can often hear them say, but our dreams are divinely inspired. Without dreams, there would be no Olympic champions; without a dream, the Wright brothers would never have attempted flight. Without a dream, the book you are now reading would never have been written.

Our dreams are God's gift to us. The manifestation of our dreams is our gift to each other. We came to this life for two reasons: to serve each other and to love each other. We didn't come here to do our own thing in isolation. We owe it to ourselves and each other to dream and to dream big. We owe it to each other to take our dreams and use them to improve the lives of those around us. It is not about pride; it is not about envy; it is not about getting ahead. It is about our dreams in action to help, serve, and protect each other. I need you to dream, I need you to manifest your dreams so I can receive your gift, and you need mine.

Some people hate the idea of sitting still, studying or reading a book. These are earth people. They would rather be active even if they don't know what they are doing or why. The way they see it, whatever they need to know, they will learn by doing. Others are a ball of energy. These are fire people. Just being around fire people is enough to wear most people out. Zeal and passion is a natural state for them. Air people are thoughtful and deliberate or deliberating. They are also decisive.

We each tend to favor one element over the others; we are each more comfortable doing what one element represents more than the others. The challenge is to grow outside of that comfort zone so that we are equally comfortable with each of the four elements. Only then can we achieve the balanced and happy life that we were born to live.

In astrological terms, fire sign people are passionate. Earth sign people are practical and "down to earth." Air sign people are thinkers, problem solvers; they have well thought out ideas. Finally, water sign people are about emotion, dreams, and intuition. These are the strengths of the elements generally speaking, but a strength to an extreme or to the exclusion of other attributes is a weakness. Passion without direction will quickly fizzle out just as dreams without action will die.

I must work hard to keep the other elements in balance with water. I love the water, I love imagining and dreaming more than doing and that is why I have not achieved all that I want to achieve. But I have learned, and I now know the importance of making a decision (air), fueling my passion (fire), and working hard (earth) to make my dreams a reality.

Water is where your possibilities lie beneath the surface of the sea. The ocean is limitless, deep, mysterious, and exciting. It is fun to dream, to imagine the possibilities. It is not so much fun to take action, face rejection or failure. Still, for those who love to dream, we must discipline ourselves to spend less time dreaming and more time doing (earth). We must be "grounded" in the real world, not a world that denies our dreams, but one that offers us the opportunity to realize the fulfillment of the dreams upon which we are willing to take action.

Water teaches us to be still and reflect. Reflection, dreaming, is not a one-time event but an ongoing activity. You will find dreams that inspire you as you dip your proverbial cup into the water, but you will need to make return trips to keep your inspiration alive.

Dreaming is a beautiful euphoric state for me, but if I choose to live only in my dreams, I will miss the opportunities of the present moment. My life is not in the future, a future I imagine for myself, nor is it in the past, however sweet my life history may have been. Life is happening now, right now, as you read these words. Your present state is all you own, and all that matters.

I was ill for one year, very sick. I didn't think I would recover. I wasn't sure if I would ever be able to hold a steady job again until a coworker and dear friend said, "David, stop waiting until you feel better to return to work. Instead, take it one moment at a time. Worry only about getting through this moment right now and let the future moments take care of themselves."

I took her advice. I returned to work sick. On many days I was late or left early, but I made an effort, not for the day but only the moment at hand, and I slowly regained my health. It took almost a year before I was fully functioning, but if I had focused on the long-term objective, I never could have obtained it. I had to focus only on what I could accomplish in the here and now.

The gift of dreams is that they inspire us. The problem with dreams is that they take our focus from the task at hand. If you focus exclusively on your dreams, your future, you may miss the opportunities in the here and now. You need your dreams, but you also need to remain grounded in the present. Life is about balance, and the elements teach us this.

The elements are interdependent, and without balance between them, no life would exist on earth. As I considered this book and how they work in my life, I opted for the order of water, fire, air, and earth not because it is right or the only way but because this is how I generally experience their operation in my life.

I dream first. I almost always start with a dream or vision

for where I want my life to go, what I want to achieve, or who I want to be. With that vision in mind, I either experience the energy of fire and enthusiasm, or I don't. If I don't experience at least a little fire, the dream will not last. If I do, then I create a plan. Plans are the domain of air and reason. After a plan is made, it is time to get to work creating my dream. Hard work is the domain of the earth. Hard work is gritty, the earth is gritty, and without grit, our plans cannot succeed.

As you dream of your future, do not dismiss anything. People need what you have to offer. You were born with a mission that only you can fulfill. If there are not many people doing what you are dreaming about, it is probably because you have not shown them the way. Ask your God or your guides to bring you those that will benefit from your product or service.

> "Every creator painfully experiences the chasm between his vision and its ultimate expression."
> –Isaac Bashevis Singer

Dreams are lovely, but as you travel the long road to dream fulfillment, that initial dream seed will almost certainly be modified. As you learn and grow, your vision will change.

When I started in magic, I wanted to do grand illusions on a full stage. I did that kind of show for ten years, but now I work alone out of a briefcase.

My vision changed, not only because of new circumstances, but also because of changing values. I enjoy mentalism far more than I ever enjoyed doing grand illusions. When

I started, I didn't know about the existence of mentalism as an alternative performance art. I learned about it as I grew in the art. The final step was necessitated when my partner left the show.

Sometimes the most adverse circumstance can bring the best long-term result. When Jill told me she was leaving I was heartsick. I had spent a fortune creating the show we were performing, and we had spent ten years perfecting our craft. For a time, I tried to replace her. I ran advertisements, interviewed candidates, and even rehearsed with some top prospects, but in the end, Jill was irreplaceable. It was time for a new direction, a new dream, a fresh vision. I didn't want to give up performing, but with a house full of grand illusions and no partner, my performance prospects were bleak.

It was then that I discovered an expert in the area of mentalism, Richard Osterlind. Osterlind published a series of instructional materials designed to help budding mentalists. I studied his material for weeks, expanded to other works, and eventually put together a show.

I had spent decades in conventional magic. I knew my material, and I knew the reaction I could get from an audience. Mentalism was a total departure for me. All the material in my act was untested. Imagine the apprehension I felt when I went out to perform my first show as a mentalist. Imagine the thrill when that show worked, when audiences responded positively, when I learned I could entertain as a mentalist.

I started in magic, carrying a box load of props. This eventually grew to a truckload. It would take three people three or four hours to set up the show for a performance.

Today, I carry a briefcase and a sound system. It takes me one trip from my car to set up the show. My focus has also changed. Mentalism is much more interactive than conventional magic. To be a good mentalist, you must be good with people. I find I enjoy it more because it is less about theater and more about that interaction.

Another important point that I would like to make about my magic and my ministerial careers is that I have never at any time in my life thus far served in a full-time capacity in either career field. Yet, I consider myself a professional in both areas. This is a significant point because, in a balanced life, which in my opinion, is a happy life, you don't need to put all your eggs in one basket. I realize that this philosophy runs in the face of most motivational or career self-help books, but it has worked well for me. I enjoy the benefits of careers in both ministry and magic, and yet I don't suffer the negatives of those careers if those careers were my full-time profession.

I consider myself an eclectic creative. I love to create in a variety of ways. I don't restrict my creative efforts to only one area, and I don't limit my eclecticism to only creative efforts.

My faith, for example, has changed and evolved.

I left the Assemblies of God and became Catholic. Many of the things I have done have been frowned upon by traditional Pentecostals and fundamentalists. Had I chosen to make a living pastoring in the Assemblies of God, I would never have enjoyed the freedom to explore the tangents that have brought such happiness and fulfillment to my life.

As for magic, I enjoy performing, and I can be more generous in my negotiations and more selective of my venues than I would otherwise be if I depended on magic income for my financial substance.

I am not sorry that I do not earn my full time living from magic or ministry. It is what is best for me, and I am glad it worked out that way.

My point in sharing these details with you is that your dream will change and evolve, and as it does, you will change and evolve. You will learn about who you are, your strengths, preferences, and desires. Change is a natural process, so by all means, embrace it. If the exact vision you had in your head at the beginning of the journey doesn't come about, it doesn't mean that you have failed. Often it means that you grew and embraced your personal growth as the vital part of your journey that it truly is.

It is sad but often true that we need a good swift kick to get us out of a comfortable nest and flying. You might resent the person or circumstances that necessitate change, but the universe is intelligent, and it knows what is best for you even if you don't.

Change allows you to dream again, to create a new, better, more mature path. Embrace change, embrace the opportunity to dream again.

"You can't build a reputation on what you intend to do."
–Liz Smith

Dreams are lovely, but they are dreams. A dream is a vision, a goal, an intention. Of itself, a dream can inspire you, it can make you feel good, but like an unplanted seed, it cannot sprout into your reality without air to nurture it, fire to fuel it, and the hard work and determination of the earth to finally bring it about.

> "Dreams are like stars...you may never touch them, but if you follow them, they will lead you to your destiny."
> –Unknown

Destiny is an odd, elusive, and sometimes frustrating thing. I have always believed in destiny. By destiny, I mean the sense that I was born with a specific purpose or mission to fulfill. My life has been mainly about finding and living that mission.

When I was in seminary, a favorite teacher used to say, "Life is Arminian when we look into the future, but Calvinist as we look back in our past." What he meant by that is that as we look at the road before us, it is filled with options, challenges, and choices we must make.

So often, we choose one road to the exclusion of another. As we look into our future, it can feel like we could so easily miss our destiny, and yet when we reach a vantage point and look back, we can usually see the hand of destiny in our lives. We recognize that all those seemingly random choices conspired to bring something magnificent in our lives, something we couldn't have planned or dreamed.

Jacobus Arminius was about choice and free will. John Calvin was about predestination and destiny. It is not an either/or but a both/and. We are free to determine our path, and yet we will find that we have been walking in our destiny all along. So, don't get hung up in the age-old question of, "What is my destiny?" Instead, focus on the present moment choice, make sure the choices you make right now reflect your values and dreams as you understand them in the moment, and trust that the universe will conspire to create your destiny because it will.

How do you extract from the sea of possibilities only the goals that are right for you and for this time in your life?

Envy is generally not looked upon as a positive emotion. Still, every negative has a positive, every argument has a counterargument, and even our darkest emotions can serve a redemptive purpose. Envy is an excellent guidepost; it almost invariably points us in the direction of our true desires. If you don't know what you want at this time in your life, ask yourself, who or what do I envy?

Instead of being jealous of the person who has what you want, plot a course to make this desire a reality in your own life. If envy inspires you to do that, then a dark emotion has served a redemptive purpose.

Another way you can learn to identify what you most value is by paying attention to your feelings. What makes you feel the most alive? By alive, I mean out of space and time. You cease to care about what time it is or where you need to be. You are fully engaged in the moment, and when that moment passes, you feel energized. Whatever it was that you were doing at that moment is probably what you were born to do.

Realign with your passion. We are spilling over into fire here a little bit, but the elements are interdependent. We need them to work together in harmony in our lives if we are to walk in our full potential.

Are you excited? Are you filled with energy and enthusiasm? If not, then maybe you have not found your passion.

Water is where you look for it; fire tells you that you found it.

Trust your impulse and your intuition. Follow your bliss and chase after what excites you. Keep gazing into the water of dreams and imagination until you find it.

As you gaze into a bowl of water you see things. The ancients called this "scrying." For our purposes, your vision is born of water. Your purpose or life mission flows from your vision, and vision emerges from water.

How do you find your vision?

What are you trying to create?

What do you get excited about creating?

God is creative.

Some believe that God created all that is in less than seven days. When we create, we partner with God; we become what God intended for us to become—co-creators.

> "Try not to become a man of success, but
> rather try to become a man of value."
> –Albert Einstein.

This is one of my favorite quotes. I keep a paper goals sheet in my pocket to remind me of the goals I intend to achieve. For many years, this quote has been at the top of my goals list.

Water will conform to the size of any container that holds it.

Water people tend to be conformist, people-pleasers. We want to make other people happy, and we will often do that to the detriment of our hopes or dreams. However, water people can choose the container that holds them; we can choose or shape our social environment. We need to consciously surround ourselves with affirming people, with people who share our dreams and passions. When we come into the company of those in opposition, it is too easy to comply, shut down, or give up. Therefore, it is in our best interest to separate ourselves from those who don't share our vision. We all need cheerleaders; emotionally sensitive people need them most especially.

Suppose you find yourself surrounded by people who will not or cannot affirm you, then, by all means, keep your dreams and visions to yourself. Conviction is an inner desire to make a change in your life, and it is highly motivating. Condemnation is someone else's judgment about your experience, and condemnations are highly discouraging, creating, in some cases, paralysis. If you have surrounded yourself with judgmental people, please consider a new social environment. It may be painful to separate yourself from some people in the short term, but in the long run, you will reap the rewards of finding an affirming social network.

Matthew 7:6 says, "Give not that which is holy unto the dogs, neither cast ye your pearls before swine, lest they trample them under their feet, and turn again and rend you."

You get to choose your dream, and you get to choose the people with whom you share it. Choose wisely.

ACTION STEPS

CHOOSE A DREAM.

My focus tends to be vocational.

I have been a human resources director for 26 years. I think in terms of professions and careers both part-time and full, but your dream may not be vocational. Maybe you want to advance in your career, or perhaps you have other priorities. Perhaps you would like to meet your special someone or start a family. Maybe you have a fitness aspiration. Perhaps you would like to finish the Boston Marathon, write a book, or earn a degree.

You can have as many dreams as you want, but the more dreams you have, the more diluted your focus will be. Concentrated focus is one key to success.

One of my heroes, Zig Ziglar, often spoke of seven spokes of a wheel. Zig taught that to be truly successful, you must devote sufficient attention to each of the seven spokes. The spokes are mental, spiritual, physical, family, financial, personal, and career.

Zig had the best approach for healthy living I have ever seen. Though he has since crossed over, he continues to be my favorite motivational speaker. This book is about finding balance and harmony between the energies of the elements in your life. Zig's system is about finding balance in these seven major areas of life.

For optimal living, you need dreams and goals in all seven areas. It would be best if you devoted some time and attention to each, but for now, choose one of the seven major areas, then dream big, visualize, think about it when you walk or shower.

You will eventually dream dreams and set goals in all of Zig's seven spokes, but for now, I want you to taste success. I want you to see and experience the effectiveness of the elements of success. Once you have experienced success in one area, you can quickly parlay that success into the other six spokes of the wheel.

In which of the seven areas do you want to concentrate?

What do you want in this area of your life?

Search your soul until you find one dream that ignites your passion, your "fire."

Once you find that dream, you are ready for the next element.

Oh yes, one more thing—write it down.

AREA OF CONCENTRATION

My area of concentration is
___
___
___
___

What do you want in this area of life?
___
___
___
___
___
___
___
___
___
___
___
___

FIRE

*"If necessity is indeed the mother of invention,
then perhaps passion is its father."*
–Dale Bredesen, MD

WE DREAM, AND OUR DREAMS inspire. Inspiration is the fuel that will keep us going when others quit.

Fire emerges from water and is the realm of passion and energy. It is also like gasoline to a car. When you run out of it, you don't go anywhere.

The fire in our gut is our driving passion. It is the fuel that will propel us toward our goal. Without passion, there is no fuel, no energy, no drive. Without fuel, the rocket sits on the launch pad indefinitely. If the goal you decided on doesn't inspire passion, if you don't want to do it so badly that you are willing to devote your spare time and attention to it even if it doesn't pay off, then choose another goal. The amount of energy you experience when you reflect on your goal will likely determine the probability that the target will eventually be achieved.

"The more intensely we feel about an idea or a goal, the more assuredly the idea, buried deep in our subconscious, will direct us along the path to its fulfillment."
–Earl Nightingale

In his letter to the Philippians, Saint Paul said that, "I have learned, in whatsoever state I am, therewith to be content." And yet, he was arguably the most ambitious evangelist of his time; perhaps of all time. While it is true that there is no moment but the present moment and that if we are not happy in this moment, nothing outside of ourselves will ever change that, it is equally valid that we incarnated for a reason, a purpose, a mission.

Once again, we must learn to balance. We must seek equilibrium between what is and what could be. We must learn to be at peace and content with what we have, who we are, and what we have achieved without letting our fire burn out. In short, we must stay hungry without sacrificing the joy that can only be ours when we focus entirely on the present moment, smelling the roses, as the saying goes.

Concrete, measurable, written goals help me maintain the balance between the already and the not yet. A written goal is a fantastic thing because it allows the freedom to focus on the here and now. That goal will be there staring me in the face as often as I look at it, and my goals are framed over my computer monitor in my office, so I look at them frequently. They also serve as a constant reminder of what lies ahead.

> "Nothing great in the world has ever been accomplished without passion."
> –Georg Wilhelm Friedrich Hegel

What is your passion?

What makes you get out of bed and get busy even when you are sick with a cold or flu?

THE ELEMENTS OF SUCCESS

If you haven't found it yet, keep looking and know that you will. Every person without exception has at least one passion.

Fire and air are beautiful compliments.

My wife and I were enjoying our fireplace recently on a cold winter night. We both noticed how bright and full the fire was. Outside there was an unseasonal nor'easter raging with 60 mile an hour wind gusts. Those gusts were forcing air down the chimney, fueling the fire and pushing the warmth from the flame well into our den.

We will discuss the significance of air in a moment, but air represents reason, thoughts, and common sense. Passion in balance is a powerful force. A passion out of control is a destructive wildfire leaving misery in its wake. Temper your passion with common sense, and you will find success in due time without sacrificing friends, family, or your 401K.

Another very down to earth way of looking at passion is excitement. When you are excited about something you forget about time. If you are really happy, you might have the sensation that you have stepped outside of time. The present moment is alive, on fire, and all-consuming.

Without passion, you will likely not take action. Use the fire in your gut to get going, do something, anything, as long as what you are doing moves you closer to and not further from your goal, the dream that water gave you.

Passion inspires action.

No passion, no action.

Know passion, know action.

The best part about action is that the more you take, the more you get. As you take one step toward your dream, you will see the next. Had you taken no action, you would never see the next level.

The future remains a blur until you step into it.

Passion will give you the energy you need to create the habits that will bring you success.

Passion creates action, action creates habits, and healthful habits create success. Passion is the rocket fuel that will get your rocket into orbit. Once in orbit, habit or inertia will keep your vessel moving toward its destination.

Archery is another of my many passions. When I was a kid, my dad joined an archery club. I spent many beautiful summer days walking through the woods of that club, shooting at targets nestled amidst tall trees.

At a young age, I learned to shoot recurve. At present, recurve is the only acceptable bow for Olympic competition. If you are not familiar with the difference between recurve and compound bows, a recurve bow has limbs that curve or curve again, thus, the term "recurve," away from the archer. The archer must use his or her strength to pull the bow back for a shot. A compound bow relies on a pully system. This system allows for more power and accuracy, and compound bows are smaller and easier to manage than recurve.

For a time, I left the sport but rediscovered it as an adult. I loved recurve, but I found that I preferred compound. My original vision was to be a recurve shooter, but as I grew in the sport, I found I was better suited for compound. We need to be open to this kind of adjustment with any dream we chase. As we grow in the field, we will evolve and change.

Once I decided that I wanted to compete, I began to read every book I could get my hands on, and I contracted with any coach who would have me. In college, they used to call that a literary search. The idea was to know what the current literature said about your area of interest. If you want to contribute to any field, you must know the contributions that have already been made so that your contribution will be truly unique. I highly recommend that you read every book you can get your hands on about your area of interest. You cannot innovate until you have a handle on the current level of understanding in your chosen field, and in most cases, only those who innovate excel.

One of the books I read on archery was *Winning Archery* by Steve Ruis. The book is indispensable if you aspire to become a competitive archer. At one point in the book, Ruis made a rather profound comment that I knew immediately had implications well beyond archery. He said, "As progress is made, the bar is raised a little at a time until either the goal is met, or you run out of passion for the task."

Please read that quote again and think about what that means, not only for sports but for any goal. You either have the passion for persisting through the grind to get to the top, or you lose interest in the goal. It is okay to run out of passion for the task, but if you always run out of passion before your goal is achieved, you may end up regretting lost opportunities.

Time goes by quickly, and before you know it, you have fewer options in front of you. So, do it now, whatever "it" is for you. Don't wait for the opportunity; create one if none exists. Don't assume you will have time or resources tomorrow that you don't have today. I know there are dozens of reasons why the present moment is not the right moment to work on your dream, but not a single one of those reasons is as compelling as your need to put your hand to the plow.

None of us are promised tomorrow. The only assets we have to work with are the ones we hold in our hands today.

My dad had a rule, and as long as I lived under his roof, I followed his rules. Once I set my hand to accomplish something, he wouldn't allow retreat. As an example, I played three years of Little League football. When I reached high school, I went out and made the team. I was and still am 5' 4" tall and roughly 125 pounds. The average height and weight of my high school team were considerably greater. I was the smallest person on the team by a wide margin.

I am not sure exactly how a person my size ever made that team, but I did. I was knocked unconscious on more than one play, and that was in practice. In Little League, small people were not uncommon, but high school ball was a little more severe, and a tiny person like me faced challenges not faced in Little League.

I wanted to quit, but my father forbade it. He told me that I had to, at the very least, finish the season, so I did. I came home bruised and battered every night. I improved as the season went on, and I contributed to my team, but it was clear at least to me, if not to my coaches, that football was not my calling.

Later in the spring, I went out for and made the gymnastics team. I spent the rest of my high school days in a sport that was much better suited to me than football. I competed well, I enjoyed myself, and I accomplished much.

No one in my family had ever been a gymnast. My dad was embarrassed. He was a lacrosse player, and gymnasts simply weren't manly enough for him. I will never forget the day he came to practice. Good gymnasts make it look easy, and he made the mistake of thinking it was easy. He hopped up on the rings, his pants fell down, and he pulled a muscle in his arm. He never criticized me again for wearing tights.

Your life is happening now. There are no refunds on wasted days, and once wasted, you cannot get them back. If you want to be, do, or have anything, the very best thing you can do is take a step, any step, no matter how large or small, toward attaining that goal.

ACTION STEPS

AT THIS POINT, YOU SHOULD be filled with energy and excitement. As the saying goes, you should be "chomping at the bit" to get started. That energy is fire; it is passion. It is what you need to move forward. If you don't feel it, then go back to your pool of dreams and keep looking. Passion gets us moving in the direction of our dreams, but a good, well thought-out plan gives us the roadmap for success. Use the energy of fire to propel you through the analytical phase of air. Fire is the fuel in your gas tank, air is the roadmap in your glove compartment.

Let that fire move you to action. Act now, don't wait, get moving, and as you progress, you will learn more about who you are and what you want. Your goal may evolve, it may change, and you may eventually abandon it. It is okay to leave a goal when you discover that the goal is not right for you, but don't give up on your dream because it is hard. The struggle to achieve your dream builds character. Even if you never succeed, if you never achieve your dream, your character will go with you into eternity, and that is real success.

Never abandon a goal because of an obstacle, but never

cling to a goal that doesn't suit you. Sometimes it is hard to discern between what we think we want and what is best for us. Knowing which goals will satisfy and which will only frustrate is a journey of self-discovery that requires time, effort, intuition, and a keen ability to pay attention. All of this will come in time, but now, feel the fire inside of you and act on it.

WHAT ACTIONS CAN YOU TAKE TO MEET YOUR GOAL?

AIR

*"Commitment is doing what you said you would,
long after the mood you said it in has left."*
–George Zalucki

COMMITMENT IS MUCH EASIER WHEN you have a clear and concise plan to follow.

The initial burst of energy that fire gives us will likely wane over time, but if we have created a clear path to success, we can execute even when we are not inspired to perform. Passion may ebb and flow, but a good plan diligently followed will see us through the rough spots on our journey.

Air is about discernment, decision-making, and planning.

You have enjoyed dreaming about what you want to have, do, or become. At least one of those dreams has ignited your passion. You are ready for action, but what action? And is the dream you are focused on really doable? Air calls us to think about and evaluate our dream. For many entrepreneurs, this is the stage of the business plan.

If you are a dreamer like me, the moment you hear the phrase "business plan," your eyes gloss over, and your mind drifts. Business plans can be complicated. Excel spreadsheets, research, and number crunching are typically associated with the business plan. Still, the short story is this: a business plan is a strategic plan for your business, no more and no less.

Suppose you feel intimidated by the concept of writing a business plan. You could speak with a small business consultant or an accountant, or you could read *Creating a Business Plan for Dummies* by Veechi Curtis.

A business plan will help you examine your business goals objectively. When you write your plan, you will ask:

- What specifically do I want to accomplish?
- Who is my competition, who is already doing what I want to do?
- What distinguishing features are my competitors offering?
- How is what I am offering different from what is already on the market?
- How much money will I need to start this venture?
- How much will I need to sustain the business until it is profitable?

I frequently speak to people who love to talk about their dreams. They are filled with passion when they speak, but when I start to drill down, it becomes clear that they don't have a plan.

I spoke with a person today who told me that he hates his day job. I asked him what he is doing to change the circumstances that he finds disagreeable. He told me that he is attending night school. He is an economics major. Attending school or otherwise furthering your education is always a good idea for its own sake, but he did not want education for its own sake. He wanted a new life.

So, I asked him, "What will you do once you graduate?" He hesitated. He didn't have a clear or specific vision for his career as an economist. I spent a little time helping him drill down, and when our conversation was over, he had decided to seek employment in the banking and finance industry.

Dreams are lovely, they make us feel good and provide the necessary fuel for our passion, but a dream without a clear and specific goal cannot change your life or anyone else's. If we are to contribute what we incarnated to achieve in this lifetime, then we must create an actionable plan, which means clear and measurable goals. Writing those goals is the domain of air.

Mary Morrissey said, "Inspiration, without action, is merely entertainment."

There is nothing wrong with entertainment, but when we dream, we see ourselves differently, in a life that we are not currently living. We cannot get to that life without a plan.

Action is the domain of the earth, and we will get to that in a moment, but air creates the plan so that the earth can then act. Without a plan, there can be no action.

"You can have anything you want, but not everything."
–Laura Lang

It is time to decide; it is time to think and plan.

What is important to you?

Air will encourage you to weigh your resources and prioritize.

Air will ask you to think about what matters to you and why it matters.

> "No life worthy of the name consists of anything more than the continual series of struggles to develop one's character through the medium of whatever one has chosen as a career."
> –Juan Belmonte.

I love that quote.

As a onetime professional in human resources, a significant part of my mission is helping people find meaning in their careers. I want engaged employees, and I want you to feel positively impacted by your work even if you are not working your dream job.

It doesn't matter what you do, but it matters a great deal how you do it. It doesn't matter if you ever find that dream job. What matters is what you bring to your work every day. Struggle is a part of every job, even dream jobs, but struggle is good because, without it, we wouldn't grow.

There are not enough hours in the day, days in the year, years in our lives to do everything we may ever want to do. We have to choose. However frustrating they may seem, our limitations are what ultimately create the character in us we incarnated to develop. The fact that we must choose one path and leave another behind forces us to evaluate our values. Our values inform our choices, and the values we hold determine the happiness or sadness, success or frustration of our lives.

THE ELEMENTS OF SUCCESS

> "Sow a thought, reap an action; sow an action, reap a habit; sow a habit, reap a character, sow a character, reap a destiny."
> –Stephen R. Covey

Intimacy with the element of air will help us develop the habit of being intentional in all we do, in every decision large and small. The more intentional and deliberate we are, the more effective our lives will become. Intention means that you understand the why, that your actions are motivated by a careful and well thought-out purpose. Air is the realm of intention. It is from the element of air that your sense of intention will be strengthened. The stronger your intention, the more effective and efficient your actions will be.

Your dreams are the gift of water; the excitement your dream generates inside you is the gift of fire. The plan you come up with to achieve what you have been dreaming about is the air's gift.

We don't have unlimited time or resources. If we did, then we could work toward every goal, but our limits force us to decide what is most important. This is why we must plan, evaluate, and reevaluate as we progress not only toward a specific goal but throughout life in general.

Air can help us answer some of the "big" questions, questions like, "Why am I attending this church or adhering to this belief system or political ideology?" Doing anything because you have always done it or because it is the only perceived option or because everyone around you is doing it is restricting. Explore, and in your exploration, become intentional. Know why you believe what you do, understand what your values are, and why you hold them. This is what an emphasis on air will do for you.

In the tarot, swords are associated with air. A sword cuts; it is precise and decisive.

Hebrews 4:12 (KJV) says, "For the word of God is quick, and powerful, and sharper than any two-edged sword, piercing even to the dividing asunder of soul and spirit, and of the joints and marrow, and is a discerner of the thoughts and intents of the heart."

We could debate what "the word of God" is, but in the passage above, it is likened to a sword, to the domain of air. Above all, it discerns and provides insight. Your "aha" moments will come as you meditate and reflect on your chosen path and the options before you. Flashes of insight will brighten your way and show you the steps you need to take. What may seem daunting will suddenly become doable in the light of genuine insight. Throughout the ages, people have believed that this level of insight comes from God, that there is a spiritual component.

Proverbs 3:5-6 (KJV) says, "Trust in the Lord with all thine heart, and lean not unto thine own understanding. In all thy ways acknowledge him, and he shall direct thy paths."

Direction for our path is what we need from the element of air.

I have often wished for multiple lives to pursue multiple lifetime goals, but I am now glad for the limits on my time and resources. If I had unlimited time and unlimited resources, then I would never have to decide what matters to me, and what matters to me defines me. I get to choose who I am, who I want to be, and who I will become. I make this decision by choosing where to devote my limited time and resources. This decision is the domain of air.

There is no right or wrong answer, there is only your answer, but your answer will tell the world, time, and eternity, precisely who you are.

What do you want for your life?

What statement do you want to make?

Who do you want to be?

Dare to have big dreams.

Which will you work on first?

My mother had a lingering illness before she crossed over. One evening as I sat with her in the hospital, I asked her, "Mom, if you could do anything and knew you could not fail, what would it be?"

I hoped to discover something that maybe I could help her do or achieve while we still had time. Her answer surprised me. It taught me a lesson about living that I will never forget.

She said, "I want to cook for my boys."

I said, "Mom, maybe you didn't understand the point of my question. I am looking for that one thing that you always wanted to do."

Mom said, "Cooking for my family is what I always wanted to do."

My mother devoted her life to my brother, my father, and me. She gave me the foundation of love I needed to pursue my dreams. She championed my causes and encouraged my growth and exploration.

Even in the area of religion, my mother wanted what was best for me, and what was best for me was my path. She was a devoted Christian and yet when I struggled with the faith in my teen years, she told me, "I want you to be confirmed so that you understand the basics of our faith, but after you are confirmed, if you still want to explore other faiths you have my blessing."

I was confirmed, and I left the church only to return to it wiser and with a greater appreciation of Christianity. I might never have made that journey if her love wasn't her north star, her guiding principle.

Sometimes we choose love.

Sometimes the interests and dreams of those we love are our primary passion.

My mother was a happy person. Her dream was the happiness of her family. Her dreams came true because of her love and devotion. You don't have to be the star or the great achiever. You only have to follow your heart.

Air encourages us to slow down from the fiery energy of our passion and think.

"Pesky common sense," as my insurance agent calls it, is the domain of air, and to the extent we choose to cultivate it, we will have happy, healthy, successful, and balanced lives.

It is our common sense that encourages us to slow down, to resist haste and think or plan strategically. Common sense tells us that we never have to be desperate; we never have to have anything; it is the bridle in the wild horse's mouth. If we never let our dreams run ahead of our common sense, then our plans will always be measured and deliberate, and our success will come in due time after steady, persistent effort.

Once, while in undergraduate school and working nights and weekends, I told my father I wanted to quit my job or quit school so that I could devote more time to my writing.

He looked at me and said, "Why aren't you writing now? Do it right now. Oh, and don't quit your day job or drop out of school."

Of course, I would have had more time to write if I had quit my day job or school, but had I made that choice I might not have two graduate degrees today, I might never have met my wife in undergraduate school, and I would have had considerably fewer financial resources.

Common sense. We all need it when we chase our dream.

Air urges us to be conservative in the pursuit of our dreams.

"Don't quit your day job," is the advice of an air-oriented person, and I am not one to quit a good job too soon. Still, there are two monumentally essential elements needed if you are to be happy regardless of where you work: You must identify with the company mission and you must like your coworkers. That said, I have never had a work experience that wasn't educational. I have learned something about succeeding in business, or I have learned something about who I am from every job I have ever worked, including the one-time gigs.

Zig Ziglar said, "Unrealistic expectations are the seedbed of depression."

To that, I would like to add despair and disillusionment.

I read a good many self-help books. I love them. I love the energy I feel when I read them. Most tell the reader to "go for it," but in the absence of a solid business plan and good old fashioned common sense, going for it can leave a person financially and spiritually bankrupt. I, too, believe that every one of us should follow our passion, but there is a difference between taking a calculated risk and a blind leap.

If at all possible, set the bar within a carefully calculated reach. Then, and only then, take the leap.

Air is prudent, wise, deliberate, and cautious. Passion leaps, air asks for evidence. Air is practical and discrete. Passion is extravagant. Air is frugal. Air is also temperate. Air will urge you toward self-restraint where passion will throw caution to the wind.

Air is the balance to water and fire.

If anything is possible, is everything prudent?

As you decide which of your dreams to pursue, which to invest in, and which to discard, think about who you want to serve. Sometimes the best in life comes from our audience, the group of people that we love, rather then what we do.

If your dream has a social component and most do, it will draw you toward people you love and respect, people you enjoy being with, and people whose company energizes you. When that happens, when your quest to see your dream come true also creates your tribe, your happiness is assured.

All work is meaningful.

My dad used to tell me, and I know he is not the only person who said this, but he said it to me first, so I will credit him with it, "It's not the work you do but the way you do it that will make the job fulfilling." Don't let some other person or some group of people define what is meaningful for you.

Only you get to decide what your passions are.

I love to write. Chances are some of you like to write, and some of you don't. I have been writing since I was old enough to hold a pen. I have dreamed of writing a bestselling novel for nearly the same amount of time.

I write every day, and I have earned money as a writer, but I am still not a professional writer.

I also love to perform. I started when I was eight, but I am not a professional entertainer.

I have enjoyed a successful career as a human resources professional. Stability in that career has given me the time and resources necessary to follow my other dreams.

It is possible to pursue what you love while keeping your day job. Only you can decide when the time is right to pursue your passion full time. It is okay if the time is never right. That, too, is your choice.

Entrepreneurs don't necessarily have more meaning in their work than those who work in larger companies. Meaningful work is a byproduct of living your mission. If you believe passionately in your company's mission, then you will likely find working there meaningful.

I am self-employed today.

I no longer have paid vacation or sick leave.

I no longer have a steady income.

I make money when I make a deal.

When I was employed, I scheduled time off to bring a book into the final stages of production or to do a show if the show time conflicted with my work schedule. I enjoyed the work I did for the company that employed me, I enjoyed the people I worked with, and I believed in my agency's mission. If you cannot say the same for the company you work for, then maybe you need a change, but the decision to leave a good day job to chance an entrepreneurial dream should be as practical as it is ambitious.

Air will teach you to create a business plan, run the numbers, and see if your idea is as viable on paper as it is in your imagination.

Are you earning a steady income from your entrepreneurial endeavor? Are your family or those who depend on you for support willing to take the chance that you are ready to adopt? Based on the income you realize at the moment from your dream job or part-time career, could you live on it?

These are the questions air asks of us. They are practical and not particularly romantic, but if we face these questions honestly, we may spare ourselves a great deal of heartache and disappointment, not to mention financial ruin.

On the other hand, you don't get do-overs.

I am 60 as I write these words.

This year, 2020, COVID-19 has impacted every American, perhaps every person on the planet. During the pandemic crisis, my company of 26 years hired a new executive officer. In April of 2020, our new exec started. He came in with boundless energy and enthusiasm. He wanted to make substantial changes to the agency. Few executive officers don't make significant changes, especially when they inherit severe problems as he did.

As long as I have been working, I have wanted to be self-employed. The new boss never asked for my resignation, but I knew he wanted a fresh start, and I wanted the opportunity to try my hand at self-employment.

I resigned.

The world is a much different place when your income depends on your deals instead of your salary. At times, I am frightened and wonder if maybe I was a bit insane to make the choice. Then I make a deal, the money comes in, and I feel more alive than I have felt in decades. I sleep better, feel better, and my thinking is clear.

While I was employed, I sponsored conventions, taught

classes, wrote books, and performed magic and mentalism shows.

Whatever it is you want to do, find a way to do it now. You don't have to quit your day job as I did, but you shouldn't put off anything you want to do. Make a plan to accomplish or achieve what you dream about and get started immediately.

We simply are not promised tomorrow. I have said this before and will likely repeat it. Today is the only moment we have. Don't let the sun set today before you have taken at least one small step toward your dream.

Some people are naturally inclined to see the most natural path to success. Not me. If there is one road with more challenges than any other, I will find it. If there is one goal more impossible, then the next, I will select it.

I know accountants, lawyers, and insurance people who look at my plans or goals and almost immediately suggest a path to reach them that strikes me like an epiphany. Why didn't I see it? But these same people would never dream my dreams. The practical people of the world don't want to be writers or speakers or entertainers. They don't sponsor conventions, knowing that there will not be any profit from that sponsorship. The dreamers do these things, and eventually, the dreamers are the ones who publish books.

This is why we need balance, why we need the energy of all the elements in our lives, and if we cannot find that balance within ourselves, then we would be well advised to seek the counsel of people wise where we are not so knowledgeable.

As I mentioned, I used to produce conventions. One year, I found myself struggling to pull one together. The venue I had selected required an insurance policy that most venues provided, but this venue expected me to obtain it. Without insurance, I couldn't use the venue.

I consulted my agent. He searched for a company that would underwrite the policy. He couldn't find one. Over breakfast, he said, "Too bad that pesky common sense is getting in the way."

I had produced two successful conferences before, but the insurance requirements in this particular year were a significant obstacle, and I was running out of time. The venue wouldn't allow me to produce the event without insurance, and no insurance company would underwrite it. At my event the previous year, I met a man who wanted to produce. I reached out to him. It was too soon for him to get it together for that year, but the next year he picked it up, and he has continued to produce events each year since.

Obstacles are always opportunities, so dig deep, access your resolve, and fight back. Your heart will tell you when to fight and when to re-evaluate, re-assess, and decide if the road you are on is the right road. Your heart will tell you what your mind fails to comprehend. Listen to your heart, and you will rarely go wrong.

Of all the elements, I find air the most challenging, yet if I ignore air's wisdom, the consequences are most disastrous. Air encourages us to slow down and be more deliberative, to resist the temptation to allow our passion to override our common sense. Water and fire get us stirred up about a future goal. Air asks us to do the research and create a solid business plan. Making a business plan can be a sobering, even discouraging, experience. Still, the alternative is to rush in and discover only after we have overextended that we have done insufficient planning to achieve our goal. As painful and as challenging as creating a workable plan might be in the present, the consequence of not carefully planning is far worse. We need to discern right from wrong, what we want from the glamor and allure of the superficial. We need form, but we also need substance. We need to be able to dream, but we also need to dedicate our limited time and resources to achieving a dream that we will appreciate as much after we achieve it as when we first conceived of the idea.

So many wants lose their luster once we hold them in our hands. God forbid that we should dedicate our lives to a dream that, once realized, we no longer cherish.

I love Indiana Jones. As a child growing up, like George Lucas and Steven Spielberg, I was a fan of Jonny Quest, the inspiration for Indiana Jones, but Indy went so much further than Jonny Quest.

In *Indiana Jones and the Last Crusade*, Indiana must save his dying father. The only way to do that is with water from the Holy Grail. An ancient Knight Templar is standing guard over a collection of goblets. If Indy chooses wrong, it will mean certain death.

The knight admonishes him to, "Choose wisely." Take your understanding of your situation, of history, of Christ and who he was, and apply that knowledge in such a way that you make the best choice, in this case, the only correct option.

Choosing wisely brings health and prosperity, choosing hastily or foolishly brings suffering. So it is in our lives. At some point, we will enter a room full of choices, and like Indiana Jones, we will have to pause and think (air) before we leap.

Long before the age of Christ, in Ancient Greece, there was a temple to which people traveled to seek wisdom or answers. A young woman would sit above a chasm and prophesize. It was known as the Temple of Delphi. Inscribed on the frontispiece of the temple were the words, "Know thyself."

How frustrating it is to journey down a road only to discover that the road is ill-suited to your personality. It would be so much better if you took stock of who you are at the beginning rather than at the end of the journey.

You have a nature that is not my nature. No two human beings are exactly alike. Whatever time it takes, whatever the investment, the most essential starting point is an honest assessment of who you are. The success of others can inspire us, but we err if we assume our success will look like someone else's. A thorough understanding of yourself to the extent that it is possible to achieve will save you years of heartache and struggle. Air urges us to invest in an understanding of ourselves before we leap into action.

Dreams are fun and euphoric.

Air is sobering and challenging.

Air reminds us that we must decide and that every decision involves choosing one road over another. Air is like a sword that cuts away the excess and leaves only the vital. As young King Arthur pulled a sword from a stone to realize his destiny, so we must draw the sword from the stone and use it to determine our destiny.

The moment you decide, you begin to attract to your life the resources you will need to bring that goal from the intangible to the tangible, from a dream to a reality. You may marvel at how perfect the timing was. The world conspires to help those who are clear about what they want.

For years, I overextended financially on performance magic. At one point, I decided I wanted to be a stage illusionist, arguably the most ambitious and expensive subgenre of performance magic. I wanted to do the big show, and within a few years, I needed a large truck to transport my show.

Once I decided to pursue this dream, a young lady came into my life who remained at my side as my performance partner for ten years. She gave me the best opportunity to succeed.

She wasn't my first performance partner. Before her, I had a woman who didn't know she was claustrophobic until I locked her in a trunk during rehearsal. She beat on the prop until I let her out, then decided the magic biz wasn't for her.

I also worked with a young lady who wanted to do stage work, but she never overcame her fear. Consequently, when she was on stage, she clammed up, and her engaging personality never came through to our audiences.

The one who remained at my side for ten years was perfect. She had a sense of humor both on and off stage; she was hard-working and never demanded more than what I could give her. She was willing to take chances, try new things, and work very hard to help me set up a show that gradually grew to be quite large and heavy. She came to me when I decided that grand illusion was my passion.

The resources you need to live your dream will appear once you fully commit to it

In addition to pursuing a career in grand illusion, I also promoted events, gatherings, and conventions. I spent lavishly and never realized a return on my investment, at least not in monetary terms. The spiritual return was well worth it, but from a purely profit/loss point of view, those conventions were never profitable.

As a want-to-be speaker, I spent too much money on coaches and consultants who promised solutions but never delivered.

After all of these very poorly run business ventures, I read an excellent book that changed my life, *The Martha Rules* by Martha Stewart.

Stewart was the breath of fresh "air" that I desperately needed. She wrote her book to help people like me, water people with big dreams but little common sense (air). *The Martha Rules* is a guidebook for healthy success, and what I mean by healthy is that it taught me how to pursue my dreams while keeping my feet on the ground and my bank account safe.

One of the most valuable lessons I learned from her book was reinvesting a portion of my profits but never exceeding that percentage and never going into debt. She taught me to "despise not the day of small beginnings" (Zechariah 4:10), to be patient, to learn to be content with starting small and building slowly as the business's income enables me.

I have lived by her principles ever since.

She is the air my water personality needed.

While some people come into your life as an encouragement at just the right moment, there are others who seek to prey on other people's dreams. These people never think of themselves as "predators"; instead, they believe they are providing a service. You will get offers to help from consultants that will range from $1,000 at the low end to $20,000 or more. They will tell you that it is an investment in yourself, and you might even feel guilty turning them down, as if to turn one of these people down is to walk away from your dream or to declare on some level that you are not fully invested or committed.

They want you to feel that way. They depend on that feeling to earn their dollar, but saying no to excess in no way denies your dream. Working within the constraints of a budget doesn't mean you are not committed. Instead, it means you are wise in the ways of air.

Patience, effort, and hard work over a long period are the best ingredients for lasting success. A quick fix is rarely quick, never inexpensive, and rarely a fix. Air will put up a check in your system, air will object. You should listen to air.

It is within the element of air that you plan for success. The likelihood that you will succeed without a plan is so slim that it is not worth mentioning. Another critical point about planning is that plans, like goals, should be written and measurable. You need to know if you have obtained a goal. You know, because your goal was specific. Similarly, you will be more likely to execute a plan that is clear and measurable.

At this point, you have a dream, and your dream inspires passion. What you don't have is a plan or path to that goal that makes sense, and that is affordable.

Set small, measurable goals that you know you can achieve. Once you reach your goal, write another that is a little bit more ambitious. For instance, I cannot control the number of books I sell, but I can control the number of words I write daily. I cannot control what a publisher might say about my submission, but I can control the number of submissions I make to publishers.

I was in sales for a time. One lesson I learned as a salesperson is that no matter your profession, you are in sales. We all have a product or service to sell. Learning the art of selling is a crucial foundation stone of success, and it is in the domain of air.

One of my sales managers taught me that success is a numbers game. You must do the work, put in the time, and make the call if you want to succeed.

ACTION STEPS

YOU HAVE A DREAM THAT ignites your passion and energy.

You have so much power that you feel you must act; you must do something to advance toward your vision or goal. Now you need a plan.

Maybe you have no idea where to start, how to plan, or where to begin. If that is your situation, then find someone who already has what you want, contact that person, tell the person about your dream and ask for an interview, counseling, or coaching. One of the fastest ways to achieve anything is by the mentor system.

The critical action step of air is to plan.

You may or may not need a mentor, but you need a plan even if it has only one step.

Create the plan, then take the first step toward executing that plan. As you take action, be prepared to revise your plan. As you gain experience, you will learn what works for you and what doesn't work. You will learn what you like and what you don't like. Revise your plan accordingly.

I recently had a conversation with some sales and marketing experts. One was an advocate of direct mail. He said, "All the big companies do it." Another said, "No, it's all about direct contact, and the most efficient way to do that is on the phone." Still another said, "It's about networking. People only buy from people they know. You've got to join the associations, sit on the board—network."

It is really about what works for you, and what works for you may or may not work for someone else.

Make a plan.

Execute your plan.

Assess and revise.

This is the domain of air.

Written goals are vital to your success.

An unwritten goal is a wish.

A written goal is power.

The SMART goal strategy, so often cited in self-help books, was created by George T. Doran in 1981. He published an article entitled, "There's a S.M.A.R.T. Way to Write Management's Goals and Objectives." From that moment, his system has been one of the most referenced goal setting systems on the planet. It is referenced so often because it works.

Take the action step of setting your goals on paper. When you do, remember the SMART system:

S = Specific

Setting the goal to "make more money" is not specific.

Setting a goal to increase gross profits by 12% within the next six months is.

M = Measurable

The more specific your goal is, the more measurable it will be.

I write 500 words a day.

I post to at least one blog every day.

These are measurable goals.

A = Achievable

My favorite speaker, Zig Ziglar said, "Unrealistic expectations are the seedbed of depression."

If your goal is too far beyond your reach, you will frustrate yourself.

I can write 500 words every day; 2,000 is a stretch.

R = Relevant

Is the goal significant to you? Do you believe in it? Do you want it badly? Are you passionate about it?

T = Time-bound

Time-bound means you have set a deadline.

I will write 500 words by 5:00 pm.

The element of air requires a concrete, achievable plan. The element of earth executes the plan.

WHAT ARE YOUR S.M.A.R.T. GOALS?

EARTH

THE ABILITY TO TRANSLATE YOUR dreams and ideas into reality comes down to your relationship with earth.

Earth is about effort, determination, and grit. Earth is about having the courage to stand your ground amid adversity, hardship, or naysayers. You can have a clearly defined dream (water) that energizes and inspires you (fire). You can have a well thought out plan (air), but unless you are willing to persevere with hard work and effort, overcoming every obstacle life can toss your way, then your dreams will likely remain dreams.

The earth is where the rubber meets the road; it is where dreams become real. No goal, however noble, was ever accomplished without hard work and effort.

The earth is gritty, the earth is dirty, and the earth is often harsh and unforgiving. Like the tarot's fool, we embrace our dream and leap into a chasm. If the fall doesn't kill us, we get up, brush ourselves off, and begin our journey. The sun beats down in the summer and makes us feel like we are suffocating. The cold winds blow through us in the winter, no matter how many layers we might be wearing. And yet, the earth is beautiful from the ocean to the mountains, on a sunny day or during a winter storm. The earth is our home, and it is breathtaking.

The earth represents our struggle to manifest our dreams.

Eden was a blissful place. Everything Adam and Eve might wish for was provided for them. When they left Eden, as we all do, God told Adam that he would "toil…all the days of your life" (Genesis 3:17). This is often described as a "curse." I don't think the curse was the toil that Adam would have to do to survive. I think it was the separation from constant communion with God.

Work is a blessing.

Consider all those who cannot work, those who are ill, and those who don't live in a nation of options about work.

We get to choose our work.

If we love the earth, we might choose to farm. If we love numbers, we might choose accounting.

Whatever our choice of work, when we do work, when we give our work our very best, we receive in return not only the monetary rewards that naturally follow hard work but also the joy and satisfaction of a job well done.

Work is not a curse.

It is a gift that we get to enjoy.

The best way to deal with adversity is to work. That is one of the gifts the earth element brings to us—the gift of hard work.

I had a colleague once who lost his adult child to disease. When I came into his office on business, he quickly swallowed the tears he was shedding.

I said, "Why don't you take a few days off? Allow yourself to grieve."

He said, "Work is healing to me."

Work is healing to us all.

The best way to deal with any problem is work. Hit the issue head-on with hard work and see how long it lasts. Hard work is more potent than any challenger. Hard work is more formidable than the meanest circumstance, and the fantastic thing is that the harder you work, the better you feel.

Taking action may not solve every problem, but no solutions can be found to any problems without work. Without hard work, there is no achievement, and there is no dream come true. You cannot find the pot of gold at the end of the rainbow if you don't go to the end of the rainbow to look for it.

In times of struggle, in times of hardship, and in times of sorrow, take action, do something, work for a better tomorrow. Prosperity and success are only dangerous if they lull you into complacency. Once the well produces water, you need to keep pumping if you want the stream to flow. The name of the 1976 Arnold Schwarzenegger film tells you everything you need to know about life on earth—*Stay Hungry*.

Keep your passions burning as long as you can, and if you feel them dying, search for the reason.

To "glory in tribulations" means to see the value in them.

Tribulations, these adverse circumstances that stand between you and the realization of your dream, are gifts from God to help you develop the character qualities that will not only see you through to the accomplishment of your dream but will also carry on with you into eternity.

Character is the only thing that matters, not what we did or what we accomplished or how much stuff we acquired, but the people we became. Make a choice right now not to accomplish something but to become someone.

The heat of adversity will create in you the fortitude, the grit, and determination that you need to accomplish your goal. Those nasty obstacles that are getting in your way are the very gateway to your success. When you learn to appreciate them for what they are, steps to becoming the best person you can be, then you will deal with each one patiently; not only patiently but gratefully.

Certainty follows action, not dreams.

As you take action, your dreams will change. As you work hard, your confidence will develop. You cannot follow a parked car, and you cannot build a life without work. As you work, some things will feel right, and some will not. Even things that felt wonderful when you imagined them might not feel so wonderful when you realize them in your life. If it doesn't feel right, change it. It is never too late, and don't fool yourself into believing you have invested too much to change. Does it make sense to hold on to something you don't like because you worked hard to get it?

Work is its own reward.

A favorite college professor of mine used to say, "You may not get a job when you graduate, but we won't take back any of your education if you don't." In other words, the time and effort you invested in your education have value in their own right.

Hard work, ease, grace, and flow are not mutually exclusive. If you don't find your hard work easy, and I know that may not make sense, but what I mean by easy is not lazy but graceful; if your work doesn't come to you with grace and ease, then maybe you are digging in the wrong field.

THE ELEMENTS OF SUCCESS

When you are working on the right dream, the process is blissful.

Be the hardest working person you know.

Never be outworked.

There may be those with more innate skills, there may be those with more resources, but if you believe in your dream, then believe also in your ability to make it happen and know that achievement and hard work are close companions.

A favorite author of mine, Peter Kreeft, said, "Politicians and business (people) must realize that the ruling purpose of the economy is not power or profit but human welfare."

It is easy to believe that because we create success, we are under no obligation to share it. We worked hard for what we earned, why shouldn't they, is too often the answer to our conscience when it taps us on the shoulder with human need. A much healthier attitude is gratitude and generosity. Let's not strive for success for selfish reasons but so that we will have the resources to help more people. Wealth should never be hoarded but shared.

Real success is more about patience, hard work, and perseverance than about the euphoria of passion. We need passion like a locomotive needs steam, but success happens when you stick to it even after you lose the thrill of that blissful goal-setting moment.

Water is the cradle of our dreams, fire is the fuel that propels us toward the effort, air gives us a solid practical plan, but earth is where our dreams become a reality. Dreams cannot become real without perseverance. The commitment we demonstrate to our goals is both an indication and a developer of our maturity and character.

We will not carry most of our achievements into eternity,

but we will take our character. It is all about character. It is not about what we have achieved or how much we have gathered to ourselves. Instead, it is about the people we become in the process. Hard work and effort builds the strong character we incarnated to create, and strong character is the only thing we will take with us when we leave this life experience.

Zoraya Tonel said, "Commitment" (some use the word maturity) "is the ability to carry out a worthy decision, even when the excitement of making that decision has passed."

Cavett Robert expressed the same idea a little bit differently when he said, "Character is the ability to carry out a good resolution long after the excitement of the moment has passed."

The excitement is the fire, fire that almost invariably burns itself out early in the game. When passion ebbs, doubts begin.

We tell ourselves that, "Maybe that wasn't a good goal after all," or, "I've changed, I'm a different person now."

You will likely face all these doubts and more as you labor for your dream.

I recently decided to study the violin.

Watching violinists create the most beautiful music I ever heard put the fire in me to do the same, but when I touched a bow to my violin's strings for the first time, I didn't hear beautiful music; what I did hear caused my pet parrot to fly from the room. It sounded like agony instead of joy, and in that moment, I realized that the road to elegant violin playing was going to be a long one filled with many hours of practice and study.

At this point, I am almost a year in. I practice every day.

THE ELEMENTS OF SUCCESS

I may not sound like Jay Ungar yet, but I am making steady improvements. I took lessons from two different professionals, and they gave me a firm foundation to build on.

I love the violin, and I play it for the joy of playing.

When I read the great writers like Ray Bradbury, I understand how far I have to go. When I see a great performer like Derren Brown, I wonder if my magic will ever reach his level. When I hear a speaker like Zig Ziglar, I wonder if I will ever have his easy charm, wit, and wisdom.

The moment you put your hand to do or be anything, you will likely realize how far you need to go to achieve the dream that so inspired (put the fire in) you. You may feel overwhelmed.

Creighton Williams Abrams, a United States Army general who commanded in Vietnam, said, "When eating an elephant, take one bite at a time."

Focus on the task in front of you, the skill you must master right now. Keep taking little steps, and eventually, you will travel the distance.

Bringing your dream into reality will be costly. You will face adversity. You will also likely fail not once but many times. Succeed or fail, you will become a better person in proportion to the effort you make.

There are no guarantees.

I wish there were.

This is why it is so important to love whatever it is that you have decided to put your hand to do. If you love what you are doing, then chances are you would do it for the joy and satisfaction the effort brings you. If you don't love what you are doing, then keep looking. You haven't found your dream yet. Most of us have to venture down many dead-end streets before we see the yellow brick road to Oz.

The purpose of passion is to fuel the initial energy required to devise a plan. Fire helps us create the habits that will place us on the path to realize that plan, but passion fades. For most people, that initial enthusiasm they feel doesn't last. When passion fades, you need resolve and hard work. Everything comes with a price, a price that we are either willing or not willing to pay.

Take a few moments to reflect on your past. If you are like me, you held a goal in your hand. It was something you wanted to do, be, or have, and yet when, on some level, you considered the cost, you decided to tuck that dream away.

Maybe you made excuses:

"It's just not the right time."

"I have too much on my plate right now."

"If I do this, I could lose my savings."

"People depend on me for financial support."

Go on, add your excuse.

I am not saying that these excuses are not valid. What I am saying is that they are excuses.

It would be best if you made a choice.

What matters most to you?

Maybe you cannot afford the risk right now. I am not your judge, and no one else has the right to be. What I want for you is to consider your options soberly and consciously. Don't merely resign your dream to an unfavorable circumstance. Instead, look the circumstance square in the eye. See if it can be dealt with in another way besides giving up on your dream.

Maybe you have children or disabled parents or siblings

to support. Does that mean that you cannot pursue your dream? No, it doesn't. You may have to work harder than the next person who doesn't have those responsibilities. Maybe you need to work at your dream part-time until you are finically able to quit your day job. Make the plan (air) and then stick to it (earth) and realize your dream (water).

Is it right to ignore my responsibilities in pursuit of my dream? No, it is not. Is it right to ignore or defer my dream to a better time? There is no better time than right now, and the only moment any of us is guaranteed is the present moment. So, what is the answer? The answer is to work on the complexity of the concerns until the solution is clear. Do what all successful people do—figure it out. There is no road map. You are in uncharted territory. There is no safety net. There is only you. Isn't that exciting? It should be.

You may have noticed my use of Bible verses throughout this book. I may not agree with every doctrine or dogma of mainstream Christianity, but I do have a love for the Bible's wisdom. Consider some of its wisdom when speaking about the value of perseverance:

> "Let us not be weary in well doing: for in due
> season we shall reap, if we faint not,"
> –Galatians 6:9.

> "We glory in tribulations also: knowing that
> tribulation worketh patience; And patience,
> experience; and experience, hope."
> – Romans 5: 3 – 4.

As Romans Chapter 5 tells us, once we have learned to

be patient, we will gain experience. With experience comes confidence, and with confidence, hope, not a pie in the sky hope but an unwavering certainty that what is not yet in your life, that dream you hope for, will in time become a reality.

Too many want it now.

Immediate gratification is the expectation of the digital age, and when that doesn't happen, the dream all too often dies, or disappointment or anger set in.

Our culture has created the expectation of immediate success.

I recently shared a meal with a real estate agent and a contractor. When I mentioned how much I enjoyed the reality shows on HGTV, they told me that many of those shows had created unrealistic expectations for real-world customers they try to serve every day. The customer expects the dream home on a budget or a massive renovation that takes only a week with no mess.

Any worthy goal requires time, attention, and hard work.

If we could get everything we want when we want it, we would miss the opportunity to grow. Trees grow after many years of too hot or too cold conditions. A goal that fails to challenge us is unworthy. All sunshine and no rain will kill the most robust tree. Set a goal you cannot reach, and then with time and perseverance, achieve it. That is a worthy goal, and you will be better for the struggle to achieve it.

There is an old Hermetic axiom that goes, "As above, so below."

The tarot's magician holds his wand pointed heavenward in one hand, and the forefinger of his other hand pointed down to the earth. Creation is a spiritual as well as a physical journey. We grow and change in the process.

As we journey toward our goal, we will meet with obstacles, sometimes in human form.

People will stand in our way; people will tell us that we cannot achieve what we dream of, and people will treat us rudely when we reach out to offer our service. If we allow the behavior of others to infect our attitude, we lose every time. You will never be truly free; you will never feel weightless or limitless until you embrace forgiveness as a lifestyle. Forgiveness is a practical and down to earth discipline that will propel your forward momentum because it will unshackle your potential.

Many books teach the lessons of forgiveness.

Most tell you to forgive others as an act of your will and intellect, arguing that your feelings will follow. I agree. But few ask you to remember to forgive yourself. Make right whatever you can, but at the end of the day, let go of whatever it is that is holding you back. Forgive yourself, let it go, and you will be free indeed to reach for the stars.

If you believe that your life could be better, you are right, but you cannot keep doing what you have been doing and expect a different result.

You need to change your behavior, even if that change is small. If you want to write a novel, for instance, you might quickly burn out if you dedicate three hours a day, but what if you write a page, or if you compose 500 words each day?

Even small steps require change. You may have to miss a television show or write when you would rather read. Creating change is the domain of earth. Until you embrace change, your dreams will always remain dreams.

Other than the refusal to embrace change, two things will hinder your progress, two roadblocks to success, two stumbling blocks that will trip up your efforts to work hard and achieve your dreams: procrastination and time-wasting habits.

Zig Ziglar used to give people a round-to-it button, and then he would tell them it was a reminder to get "round to it," to get to work. He also used to say, "If you're going to have to swallow a frog, you don't want to have to look at that sucker too long."

Whatever it is you are dreaming of, please do it now.

Don't try to stop a bad habit.

As you work toward your dream, you will discover one bad habit after another.

When you are not working toward an important goal that requires concentrated effort during so-called "off" hours, you don't notice time-wasting habits, but once you come home from work at night to work on what matters, you will find that favorite TV show a distraction. Maybe for you it is not a TV show, maybe it is something else. You probably already know what distracts and derails your efforts. Perhaps you are too tired at the end of a long day to complete one more task.

If you try to kick the bad habit through willpower, you will likely lose the battle. Instead, think in terms of replacing one option with another, make a different choice about how you invest your time. Replace a bad habit, unproductive time, with a good habit, time invested in something that will bring you closer to realizing your goal.

Jane Fulton once said, "Insanity is doing the same thing over and over again but expecting different results."

You must change, and change is not easy for anyone. Still, it is infinitely more manageable if you substitute a productive habit, one that you enjoy, for a time-wasting activity. To create a new result in your life, you must create new patterns.

> "Sow a thought, and you reap an action; sow an act, and you reap a habit; sow a habit, and you reap a character; sow a character, and you reap a destiny."
> –Ralph Waldo Emerson.

Ralph Waldo Emerson understood the relationship of the element of earth to successful living.

Our thoughts are the domain of water and air; our actions are the domain of fire and earth. Working together, they produce not only our achievements but, more importantly, our character, the very people we are, and our character not only creates but determines our destiny both here and in the hereafter.

ACTION STEPS

FIRST, YOU CULTIVATED A DREAM. The dream was meaningful enough to excite and inspire you, so you created a plan, a concrete, measurable plan for bringing your dream from the realm of imagination into the real world.

The real world is gritty and dirty. When you ask the real world to give you your dream, the real world will say no—if it acknowledges your existence at all.

Populated with critics, the real world will stand in line to tell you that you are too old or too young or too something to achieve what you want to achieve. The real world is full of conflict and obstacles, but it is also where your dream waits to be born. Each naysayer, each seemingly insurmountable problem, is a gift that will bring you one step closer to what you want.

Thomas Edison said, "Opportunity is missed by most people because it is dressed in overalls and looks like work."

Your opportunity is buried amidst all the small tasks you will need to complete each day to achieve your dream.

It is hidden in the rejection notices from publishers or employers.

It is buried beneath the inquires you will send out seeking a deal.

It is your job to find your dream amid consistent and daily hard work.

Work is the domain of the earth.

We were created to perform productive work, and when we cooperate, we feel alive.

It is time to get dirty.

Your action step assignment is to put the plan air gave you to work.

Change it if you have to but make it work, force the universe to give you what you want.

"Force" is a strong word, but it speaks to the amount of effort I am encouraging you to make. You cannot force anyone to do anything, but you will not have to when you work with force and determination. The universe will meet you halfway. Opportunities will fall into your lap. Serendipitous meetings will happen at just the right time.

The world wants you to succeed.

What are you waiting for?

HOW CAN I PUT MY PLAN TO WORK?

SPIRIT

*"For what shall it profit a man, if he shall gain
the whole world, and lose his own soul?"*
–Jesus Christ, Mark 8:36

*"The elements would scatter, and the entire
world would fall apart if they were not held
together by the mysterious fifth element."*
–Robert Place

IMAGINE YOU FIND A BOTTLE on a beach.

You rub it, and a genie appears.

The genie tells you, "I will grant any single wish but only one wish. I will make you successful at anything you choose, or I will give you love in your life, joy in living, and peace of mind that will never leave you."

Which would you choose?

Would you become a rock star, or would you choose love, joy, and peace?

At this point in my life, my mental state is more important to me than goal achievement. I once thought that goals could bring me a positive mental state, but they cannot. Achievement doesn't equate to love, joy, or peace; it is only achievement. Love, joy, and peace come from another source, the fifth element, spirit.

It is easy to believe that our joy in living is a function of our success in goal achievement, but that is not the case.

Have you ever heard the phrase, "Wherever you go, there you are"?

Some attribute this statement to the Chinese philosopher, Confucius, and maybe he said it, but the etymology of the quote is not clear. Nevertheless, the general meaning in this context is if you are not at peace now, you will not be after you achieve this or that goal.

The fifth element, and by far, the most neglected, is spirit.

Some argue that there is no spirit. They would say that there are only four elements. My concern from the beginning of this work has been to maximize each element's contributions and characteristics in your life for the highest possible quality of life. I want you to have an abiding sense of peace and wellbeing regardless of your external circumstances. I want you to thrive, to know love, peace, and joy as not only events but ongoing attributes.

I don't believe people can live optimally if they neglect their spiritual needs. It would be the equivalent of saying, "I don't need water," or, "I don't need food," or, "I don't need air." The effects of neglecting our spirituality might not be as immediate as starvation, dehydration, or suffocation, but they are equally devastating.

Spirituality has always been a high priority in my life. It never ceases to amaze me when I encounter those who have never invested time, energy, or thought in their spiritual path. I am not only referring to those who intentionally avoid any discussion of spiritual matters, because at least those people have made a conscious choice. I am primarily referring to those who have never made a conscious choice, to those who believe what they believe because they always have. These people drift along like a leaf on a stream, content to go wherever the stream takes them. That sounds romantic but in spiritual matters, as in business, choosing to be deliberate and intentional usually yields better results than being passive or trusting too much in inertia.

While I have very definite spiritual beliefs, I intend to be non-sectarian and non-dogmatic. This chapter is not intended to advocate for any particular religious ideology or point of view. However, I do feel strongly that it is in the best interest of every person to explore and evaluate the options available and select the option that best serves at the moment. I say "at the moment" because ideology can change and evolve just like anything else.

We accept that trees grow over time. We acknowledge that our children will not be the same people in ten years, five, or one, that they are today. We expect car manufacturers to make better and better cars; we move our investments to maximize our return, but when it comes to our religious ideology, fear, guilt, and tradition can get in the way of growth.

Our beliefs may change over time.

That is okay.

Growth in spirit is as natural as growth in any other area.

I believe doctrines today that I wouldn't have considered options 20 years ago. In some ways, I feel blessed that I never earned my leaving solely from pastoral work. Had my living depended on it, I might not have explored, and if

I never explored, I would never have discovered a different point of view that I like better.

Change and growth are natural and healthy in every area of our lives.

Your higher self, your soul, needs spirit the way your body needs water. The solution that satisfied your parents or your grandparents may not be the best fit for you. As in all things, trust your intuition. If it doesn't feel right, then it is not right.

Those of us who live in a free society are fortunate. Today, with internet access bringing people of like mind together from all over the world, there is an opportunity like never before.

In 2004 I discovered the Christian Goth community when I came across a web site devoted to serving the population. The reaction from most of my colleagues was that Christian and goth didn't belong together. I went on to produce two national conventions for the community, and we changed the perception of many people. While I have since drifted from that community, I made friends during that time who are as close to me as family. I would never have made these friends or even met these people if I had prejudged that the community was not right for me before giving it a fair chance.

My life has been enriched through exploration. I have a wide variety of both secular and sacred interests.

I enjoy exploring spiritual paths as I enjoy the exploration of new places or new food types. Just as travel expands your perception, so too does the exploration of spiritual paths, but in my opinion, even more so.

I had the benefit of an anthropology minor in undergraduate school. The study of people and culture had always fascinated me, so when I had the opportunity to minor in cultural anthropology, I jumped at the chance. Stepping fully into someone else's shoes is a discipline. It is not easy to set aside your preconceived ideas so that you might fully open to new ways of thinking. But the challenge is worth the effort.

In anthropology, there is a system for studying another culture. Like all science, it is analytical but what it produces is hard evidence that the world view of one culture can be dramatically different from our own. There is more than one way to look at experience, the universe, and the big questions like, "who am I?" "why am I here?" "is there a God?" and "what is God like?" We all think we know the answers to these questions and that our solutions are the "right" ones. Still, every culture takes for granted that its answers are the right ones. Until you have stepped out of your comfort zone in the area of spirituality and seen the big questions from the point of view of a culture different from your own, you are not prepared to evaluate yours or anyone else's world view.

What I am encouraging is a systematic and intentional exploration of spirituality. What I am discouraging is a "take it for granted" attitude.

When you find the spiritual path you were born to follow, you will have found your bliss, and finding your bliss is what this book is all about.

I taught an advanced class, an exegetical Bible study to some of my church's brightest and best for over 15 years. What never failed to disturb me was the tendency of those in my class to trust the pastor and the party or denominational line. In addition to the exegetical work that my students came for, I also taught them how to study, and I encouraged them to pursue questions on their own. Few took me up on my offer.

If flow is the ultimate goal, a life of purpose and meaning, we are more likely to find it in the realm of spirit then from our vocation. In a sense, when everything else flows from spirit, we are generally better connected and happier.

Flow itself is an interesting concept. While, generally, I wouldn't say I like to reference Wikipedia, it can help establish some basic cultural definitions. According to Wikipedia, flow is defined as "the mental state of operation in which a person performing an activity is fully immersed in a feeling of energized focus, full involvement, and enjoyment in the process of the activity. In essence, flow is characterized by complete absorption in what one does, and a resulting loss in one's sense of space and time." I like this definition.

Imagine waking up and spending every day in flow. You are happy, you are excited to be alive, the day passes, and you wonder where the time went. You cannot wait to get up and do it again. Life is thrilling, life is good, and you are glad to be alive. You live each moment of each day with a sense of mission, you no longer wonder if you are on the right path, you know you are. This is what I mean by a life in flow.

In Galatians 5:22, Saint Paul said that "the fruit of the Spirit is love, joy, peace..." If love, joy, and peace were constants in your life, would you be in "flow"? For me, the constant and consistent presence of love, joy, and peace is what flow is all about.

According to Paul, love, joy, and peace are fruits or byproducts of spirit. Fruit appears on a tree when the tree is in season, but even out of season fruit doesn't disappear. Without winter, there would be no spring.

The context of Galatians 5 is relationships. Paul contrasts a life that is not in flow with one that is. He argues that when we abide in spirit, when we make spirit a priority in our lives, we experience an abiding sense of not only love, joy, and peace but also longsuffering, gentleness, goodness, faith, meekness, and temperance—all qualities that contribute to our sense of wellbeing and the quality of our relationships.

In contrast, Paul argues that when we don't hold spirit in high priority, we experience envy, hatred, and strife, i.e., troubled relationships. If the foundation of love, joy, and peace is healthy relationships with spirit and with each other, the foundation begins with spirit. It is easy to get ruffled by the people or circumstances around us when we take our eyes off the bigger picture. Is this all there is, or is there something more, perhaps something eternal?

If we have an eternal perspective, then everything else is temporary.

ACTION STEPS

SPIRITUALITY IS AN INDIVIDUAL JOURNEY. Yes, there are churches, synagogues, mosques, and other formal places of worship to get plugged into a spiritual community. While the spiritual community is important, what is more important is that you fully embrace the faith that is right for you. To that end, I would offer you this:

Embrace the idea that you are a spiritual being, that you are eternal, that you have a spiritual destiny. We are immortal spirits temporarily inhabiting material bodies so we can interact with the material world. The depth of our spiritual experience often determines the quality of those interactions.

Set specific time aside to nurture your faith and your spirit. I pray every morning at dawn. In the afternoon, I take a break to reflect on my pastor's message on social media. It also helps to devote some of your vacation time specifically to your spiritual journey.

Spiritual retreats, whether at home or a retreat center, are a great way to recharge. They can help you realize that the way you usually live is not necessarily how you have to live. However, to bring more awareness into your daily life, you will find that you also need some reminders at home. This can be a short morning meditation; for instance, simply watching your breath while the coffee is brewing, or taking an hour each weekend to read a spiritual book.

Follow your heart as opposed to the crowd. Don't be embarrassed or ashamed of your path. Don't allow the dogmatic and sectarian people of the world to shame you away from your journey. If you dare to achieve any goal that has meaning to you, then have the courage to be true to your convictions.

Look for your tribe, but don't be afraid to slip in and out of tribes, and don't let your tribe inhibit your growth.

Finally, be willing to commit fully to a spiritual path, but at the same time, never be afraid to change course.

I am praying for you.

You are standing on the threshold of a happy and successful life.

CONCLUSION

As we come to the end of this book, I have a prayer for you. I pray that God will give you a vision for your life, a vision that will inspire and motivate, a vision that will draw you into a life of service. I pray that your service will fulfill and enrich both your life and the lives of those around you. I pray that you will have the faith to "believe in the beauty of your dreams" (Eleanor Roosevelt), faith to believe that you can succeed if you try and that you deserve to succeed.

Finally, I pray that you will find the courage to act and that once you put your hand to the plow, you will stick to it tenaciously until your find the success you have been dreaming of.

You can make daily choices in situations and circumstances, both large and small, that will lead you closer to or further from your dreams. Success is a habit just as overeating, or writing, or fitness, or prayer. We cultivate that habit with every choice we make throughout the day. Eventually, our choices define our character and determine who we are.

Choose to live in hope instead of fear.

THE ELEMENTS OF SUCCESS

It is okay to feel fear, but you want to make a conscious choice to be optimistic instead. Choose love over indifference, choose to care, choose to be involved rather than look the other way. That situation came into your path for a reason. Why not learn from it? Give instead of take. Be the most generous person you know.

"Look out for number one" is the slogan of an immature soul.

Success is ultimately not about how much you keep but what you give away.

Success is not defined by the things you have in your life but by the character you have built in the process of living.

It is said, "You can't take it with you," but that is only true of material things. You will take your character with you. Will you carry a character that makes you proud or ashamed? The choice is always yours to make. You make it with every decision, large and small, throughout every day.

Ultimately, it is not your goals that matter so much as the person you have become during the struggle to achieve them.

Seek to add value in whatever circumstance or situation you find yourself, and you will have discovered one of the keys to joyful living.

> "Someday, after mastering the winds, the waves, the tides, and gravity, we shall harness for God the energies of love, and then, for a second time in the history of the world, man will have discovered fire."
> –Pierre Teilhard de Chardin.

Now go out and create the life you were born to live!

ABOUT THE AUTHOR

David Dellman is an HR professional and entrepreneur with over 27 years of experience leading corporate HR teams. He is a Certified Senior Professional in Human Resources and a SHRM-SCP. David graduated from seminary with an M.Div. and holds a master's degree in an education related field.

As a magician, David has toured with a grand illusion show and entertained families in the comfort of their own living room. He currently performs a mentalism and mind reading act. He is comfortable in front of thousands or in front of ten.

David's other published works include two novels: *The Mentor's Gift* and *The Christmas Garden*. He lives with his wife Janis and their Amazon Parrot Phoebe in the Baltimore area.

For more information, please visit:
https://daviddellman.com/
https://themagicofdaviddellman.com/
YouTube channel: https://www.youtube.com/daviddellman
Facebook: https://www.facebook.com/davidjanisd

www.ingramcontent.com/pod-product-compliance
Lightning Source LLC
Chambersburg PA
CBHW021408290426
44108CB00010B/441